RELIGIOUS LIFE
AT THE CROSSROADS

RELIGIOUS LIFE AT THE CROSSROADS

A School for Mystics and Prophets

AMY HEREFORD, CSJ

ORBIS BOOKS

Maryknoll, New York 10545

ORBIS BOOKS
Maryknoll, New York 10545

Fathers and Brothers
MARYKNOLL

Founded in 1970, Orbis Books endeavors to publish works that enlighten the mind, nourish the spirit, and challenge the conscience. The publishing arm of the Maryknoll Fathers and Brothers, Orbis seeks to explore the global dimensions of the Christian faith and mission, to invite dialogue with diverse cultures and religious traditions, and to serve the cause of reconciliation and peace. The books published reflect the views of their authors and do not represent the official position of the Maryknoll Society. To learn more about Maryknoll and Orbis Books, please visit our website at www.maryknollsociety.org.

Manufactured in the United States of America

Manuscript editing and typesetting by Joan Weber Laflamme.

Library of Congress Cataloging-in-Publication Data

Hereford, Amy.
    Religious life at the crossroads : a school for mystics and prophets / Amy Hereford, CSJ.
       pages cm
    Includes bibliographical references and index.
    ISBN 978–1–62698–048–8 (pbk.)
    1. Monastic and religious life—History. I. Title.
BX2435.H47 2013
255'.9—dc23
                                                2013012229

CONTENTS

INTRODUCTION

Two roads diverged in a yellow wood,
And sorry I could not travel both
And be one traveler, long I stood
And looked down one as far as I could
To where it bent in the undergrowth;

Then took the other, as just as fair,
And having perhaps the better claim,
Because it was grassy and wanted wear.

—ROBERT FROST

It is fairly commonplace at this point in time to acknowledge
that women's religious life in the United States is at a major
crossroads and to ask where it might be headed. This book will
take up that question, examining its current reality and exploring emerging trends.

As I survey this moment in history, it seems like more than
two roads are diverging before us. Religious life is at a major
intersection with highways and byways and simple grassy
paths all stretching out before us, inviting us in dizzying variety. We can certainly see the broad path we've taken in the
recent decades: the path of renewal and a dual fidelity to the
call of the gospel and of our charisms, and to the call of the
Second Vatican Council to bring that gospel and charism to
our world with all its joys and hopes, griefs and anxieties.[1]
There are also grassy paths in want of wear that beckon with

---

[1] *Gaudium et Spes*, no. 1; *Lumen Gentium*, nos. 43ff.; and *Perfectae Caritatis*. All official church documents are available on the vatican.va website.

their simplicity, veering off in one way and another, each with the promise of gospel fecundity along with attendant risks and uncertainty.

As we stand at this place, we can turn around and look back on the roads that brought us here—roads that stretch back over millennia and over much of the globe. The earliest religious responded to the call of the gospel in a radical way. They witnessed to Christ with their blood and they fled urban centers to live the gospel simply, radically, and deliberately.

Some of the roads we've trodden in the past called forth wisdom and others holiness. Travel on many of these roads was marked by courage and creativity in the face of adversity as well as by heroism and zeal in bringing the gospel to uncharted lands and places in the human heart and to the darkest depths of human misery.

Those of us who are just now setting out on this road at the dawn of the twenty-first century are heirs to this glorious tradition. We set out with these roads at our backs, with the daunting task of bringing the gospel into this new millennium, into new generations, new cultures, and new situations. We came knocking on the doors of great motherhouses or the doors of small neighborhood homes, seeking to become a part of the great adventure that is religious life.

We hear the stories of countless sisters and brothers feeding the hungry, teaching the young, comforting the afflicted, healing the sick, visiting the imprisoned, counseling the doubtful, and doubting the certainty that frequents the halls of power. We see the system of hospitals and clinics; we see the schools, the colleges, and universities. They are brick and mortar testimony to the work of religious and to the generous collaboration of so many people in the spread of the gospel. We witness the simple daily faith of these sisters and brothers continuing to live lives of quiet courage, their hands wrinkled with age and worn with work, their hearts graced through long exposure to the words and the wisdom of the gospels. Heirs to this tradition, we take our places with pride beside our brothers and sisters.

Captured by the call that is at the core of every religious vocation, we breathe in the stories, hopes, and dreams of religious life. Thus prepared, we set out to learn the wisdom of this road, to learn the things that this road will teach us. We know that the time is upon us to take responsibility for this life, for what it is becoming and for what it will offer to succeeding generations.

In religious life we commit ourselves to God, to vowed life, and to a community forever. *Forever* is a scary and amazing thing to say. It always has been and always will be. That's why it's the subject of songs and art and poetry. It's bigger than the word and bigger than the moment of commitment. It's even bigger than the life to which we commit. It touches into the bigness of God, who is Love. It brings us all to the edge of the cliff and invites us to jump, to throw caution to the wind. It invites us to be the best of ourselves; it invites us into a godly Love.

This *forever* is particularly poignant today. Communities have an impressive story of life, ministry, and renewal, but their current members are mostly retired, and many are elderly. Increasingly, these communities are recognizing that they are in the final generation of the amazing Vatican II renewal story. They are not giving up, but they are letting go of ministries and of many of the works and institutions they have served admirably for a century or more. They know the time is right for this; it is not defeat but rather the completion of an impressive chapter in the history of religious life. It is not denial of the dream but affirmation that the dream is fulfilled. It is not dying; it is really living.

"For everything there is a season, and a time for every matter under heaven. . . . He has made everything suitable for its time; moreover he has put a sense of past and future into their minds" (Eccl 3:1, 11). As we go forward, step after step, day after day, heartbeat after heartbeat, it is hard to know when the time of fulfillment comes. Yet as way leads on to way, eventually the time comes when we have to make a change. We have to surrender to what is, to what will be, to the heartbeat of the Eternal. In wisdom, in gentleness, in silence, the God of Love whispers when it is time for the new to unfold in the heart of the old.

THE TWO COHORTS

The demographics of women religious today are striking and certainly indicative of changes to come. Anecdotally, we all know there are many elderly sisters and many fewer younger sisters. Statistically, there were approximately fifty-seven thousand women religious in the United States in 2012, but only three thousand (5 percent) of them were under the age of fifty-five. It is striking to compare the demographic curve of religious life with that of society overall (see Figure 1).

It is fair to say that there are two age cohorts in religious life today: the dominant cohort between the ages of sixty and one-hundred, and the minority cohort between the ages of twenty and fifty-nine. While no generational analysis is completely accurate, it is nevertheless fair to say that the experiences and outlook of these two cohorts are distinct.

The dominant cohort entered religious life between 1930 and 1970. They generally entered religious life with others in their entrance year and often entered in large groups. Those who entered were relatively homogeneous in age, culture, and ethnicity. Their entrance groups were often the largest their congregations had experienced in their entire history; they were the

Figure 1. Age: Women Religious/US Population Comparative Demographic Curve

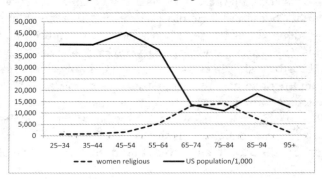

dominant cohorts from the moment they entered religious life. They received their formation within their own institutes with the others who had entered that year or in the year or so before or after them. This formation was received before, during, or shortly after Vatican II. The entire cohort experienced the turbulent years after the council and the exciting and challenging process of renewing their congregations. Deep and significant relationships in community were forged in this important time. This cohort has been sharing the life of its province or congregation for between forty and eighty years, with few new members entering but with increasing numbers dying as the entire cohort ages. This cohort now forms 90–95 percent of the community.

The minority cohort entered after 1970 in smaller groups, often alone or with one or two others. More recently there may be several years between the arrival of new members. Those entering in this cohort are more diverse at entrance in age, education, ethnicity, and cultural background. Because they enter alone or in small groups, they participate in intercommunity formation programs. They often report that they are warmly welcomed by the members of the dominant cohort in their communities. Nevertheless, they find that it is difficult to form deep bonds with these women who have established friendships, little in common with the younger women, and difficulty welcoming them as full members of the community, even after ten or twenty years or more. The minority cohort is generally only 5–10 percent of the community, and members of this cohort often report feeling unheard, or if heard, they remain a lone, dissonant voice whose ideas and energies cannot be incorporated into the life and plans of the dominant cohort. This remains true even when the community is making decisions about the future that the minority cohort will live with for another forty to eighty years. For example, in one community there are ten members under the age of sixty, but not a single one is in leadership, in formation work, or on the congregation's "futuring" committee.

Given the place of women's religious life in the United States today, with its median age nearly surpassing the life expectancy of women in this country, communities are coming to see that it is likely that they have one or two more cycles of leadership (usually four-to-six-year terms) before the matter becomes critical and there is no longer time or a critical mass of members able to make decisions, get the affairs of the community in order, and ensure the dignity of the members' final years and their legacy. Many communities are approaching their historical fulfillment as institutes; they are likely writing the last chapter of the life story of their institutes, whether they realize it or not. This will require some realistic and careful planning to prepare for this phase of the life journey and to be able to live it with dignity. This work is the work of the dominant cohort, a work that will ensure that the last chapter of the community's history is as compelling and grace filled as was the first chapter and every chapter in between. It is immensely important work, and it is necessary to ensure the legacy of the community and to ensure that members are able to make their own choices in this regard and to live this phase with dignity.

The minority cohort has a different task. We certainly love our sisters, wish to remain in relationship with them, are ready to support them in their work, and bless them on their journey. However, our task is to imagine the future of religious life in the next fifty years. We are committed to do honor to our heritage and make choices to adapt the life to the new reality in which we find ourselves.

Religious communities are a privileged place to live the gospel and share prayer and life. In communities we support one another in our commitments to an ever-deepening contemplative practice, to radical Christian life, and to service. In addition, our life together is at the service of the wider community, which we serve by prayer, witness, and ministry. In community we seek to live the values we want to bring to the world.[2]

Studies of the lifecycle of organizations speak to the present reality of our communities. Like the individuals that make them

---

[2] Susan Wilcox, "Occupy Religious Life-Action," *Mystics and Prophets* (blog), July 29, 2012.

up, communities are born and grow. They reach a certain maturity and live for a period of years or even of centuries, waxing and waning, learning, exploring, and occasionally giving rise to new life in new projects or new foundations. Eventually, each of us will age and decline, as will most of the communities of

Figure 2. Lifecycle

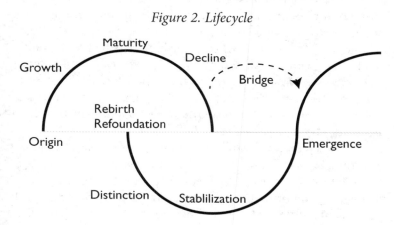

which we are a part (see Figure 2).[3] This is a natural cycle, and each stage of life has its gifts and challenges. We are most richly blessed when we engage the reality of our situation and do the task that is appropriate to it.

In institutional decline there is another reality that may also be at work. As the energies of the group wane, there may be some who set out to bring the life of the group into a new reality, a new situation, a new incarnation. This may be called *refoundational energy*. Rarely the work of the entire congregation, it is generally the few who set out to plant the seed of new life. These few feel a rising hope, and with a tenuous courage, they set out to build something new. Whispered first in prayer and among

---

[3] Margaret Wheatley and Deborah Frieze, *Walk Out Walk On: A Learning Journey into Communities Daring to Live the Future Now* (San Francisco: Berrett-Koehler Publishers, 2011), 10–15.

friends, the new energy embodies the genius of the community in a new form that has the potential of growing, stabilizing, and in time emerging as a new form of the community. Under the inspiration of the Spirit these groups can grow, and when they emerge, they can invite others to join the emerging project.

While these small projects may represent the hope of a new future of the congregation, they also challenge the group's self-understanding. They may unintentionally bring into relief the decline of a congregation when some members believe it is still viable, even vibrant. They may shine a light on the members' unwillingness to name the present situation for what it is and to address this situation. For this reason some of the projects will be misunderstood, criticized, and even opposed by the very members who may one day benefit from the new life they bring. Yet to their credit, many of these communities are eager to bless their members and support them in these projects. They listen with interest, if not always with complete understanding, as the new generation of members takes responsibility for carrying religious life into new times and places.

Sister Mary Luke Tobin, a Sister of Loretto who was one of the few women who attended Vatican II, tells the story of such moments in religious life. She explains that there will come a time when some of us will go one way and others will go another, each group remaining true to its call and living its truth. At that moment of parting, she imagines the groups will give each other a blessing and a promise of support and prayers. This is very much my hope for this crossroads in the history of religious life. This is the theme this book explores.

OVERVIEW

The first chapter traces the two-thousand-year history of religious life from the viewpoint of today's shifting consciousness. The Vatican II renewal of religious life in the second half of the twentieth century prepared us for a more fundamental reinvention of the life that will bring us into the middle of the twenty-first century. Historically, religious life has reinvented itself every five hundred years or so, with the new forms continuing to exist alongside the old.

In the early Christian centuries desert hermits, ascetics, and pilgrims sought to embrace a life of deep personal commitment to prayer and gospel living, to the exclusion of any other primary life commitment. We have writings from these fathers and mothers of the desert, who heard the call to a more radical form of life.

By the fifth century this way of life found new expression in monastic communities. Experience had shown that individual wandering monks were sometimes unruly and disruptive. By gathering in stable communities, Christians found support and challenge for the living of their radical commitment to prayer and gospel living. Benedict and Augustine wrote rules that survive to this day and continue to inspire Christian communities.

In the Middle Ages the life reinvented itself as some of the large and powerful monasteries found it difficult to maintain their fidelity to those founding ideals. The mendicants sought lives of poverty and simplicity and networked their local houses into international orders for mutual support. Franciscans and Dominicans are prime examples of this life form.

Then again, in the sixteenth century, the apostolic orders arose in response to the pressing needs of the church and of society. The Jesuits, the Sisters of St. Joseph, and many groups arose to carry out the mission of Jesus in the world. Each of these reinventions arose because of changed circumstances and the need for a new response from religious. Are the radical shifts in religious life and in the culture of today calling for yet another reinvention, a new form of the life that will not supplant the former but, as with each of the prior forms, continue to exist alongside the old?

The second chapter examines some theological sources for this task of reinvention. We can take inspiration from twentieth-century visionaries Dorothy Day, Jean Vanier, and Dietrich

Bonhoeffer, who all saw that the key to living radical Christian life in today's world is community. We seek to glean from them the threads of a theology of community that can guide us today.

Bonhoeffer writes: "The restoration of the church will surely come from a sort of new monasticism which has in common with the old only the uncompromising attitude of a life lived according to the Sermon on the Mount in the following of Christ. I believe it is now time to call people to this."[4] Bonhoeffer began to live that dream in Germany in the midst of the Second World War. It was in community that he and others found the wisdom and courage to confront the horrific situation around them. They sought to live the gospel with fidelity and courage and to challenge both church and state to stop the violence and the genocidal program of the Nazi regime. This cost Bonhoeffer and some of his collaborators their lives.

> The expansion of Christianity and the increasing secularization of the church caused the awareness of costly grace to be gradually lost. . . . But the Roman church did keep a remnant of that original awareness. It was decisive that monasticism did not separate from the church and that the church had the good sense to tolerate monasticism. Here, on the boundary of the church, was the place where the awareness that grace is costly and that grace includes discipleship was preserved. . . . Monastic life thus became a living protest against the secularization of Christianity, against the cheapening of grace.[5]

The Catholic Worker movement, following the inspiration of its founder, Dorothy Day, establishes communities of hospitality where it is "easier to be good"—places where gospel values are deliberately and systematically integrated into the life of the

---

[4] Dietrich Bonhoeffer, "A letter to Karl-Friedrich Bonhoeffer," in *A Testament to Freedom* (New York: HarperOne, 1995), 424.

[5] Dietrich Bonhoeffer, *The Cost of Discipleship*, 1st ed. (Bel Air, CA: Touchstone, 1995), 46.

community through personal commitment and regular clarification of thought and values.

Jean Vanier, founder of the L'Arche movement, believed that communities committed to gospel living could be the leaven so needed by our society:

> So many in our world today are suffering from isolation, war and oppression. So much money is spent on the construction of armaments. Many, many young people are in despair because of the danger of nuclear war. Today as never before, we need communities of welcome; communities that are a sign of peace in a world of war.[6]

Many of the men and women who are seeking religious life today long for communities that exemplify these values: a radical commitment to shared gospel living, a commitment to a balanced lifestyle where there is time for prayer, community, and mission. We seek to incarnate the gospel here and now, asking what task God might take up on moving into our neighborhood. In small local communities we become peacemakers, share the good news, live lightly on the earth, and actively pursue justice. We share life, goods, and spirituality so that we can support one another in the commitments we have made.

The third chapter explores the current place of religious life and seeks to discover the seeds of newness in this situation. There are three thousand religious women under the age of fifty-five in the United States, and these women are in about four hundred different institutes, leaving just a handful of younger women in most institutes. What is this about? Wouldn't good planning, efficiency, and sustainability require that these women be concentrated in fewer communities, so that they would be able to support one another and there would be only a few sustainable communities? Or is there something else afoot here? What is the Spirit's dream in this context?

---

[6] Jean Vanier, *Community and Growth*, 2nd rev. ed. (Mahwah, NJ: Paulist Press, 1989), 177.

Speaking with the women in the minority cohort in religious life, I find a few hints about the dream of God for the future. These are amazing women: bright, confident, articulate leaders. Yet they are so few in their communities that their voices and insights can be lost.

Another fact about this minority cohort is that its members have strong intercommunity relationships, supports, and sensibilities. They have been involved in intercommunity programs from the beginning of their religious lives, and they maintain strong relationship with women religious in other institutes. One organization that supports these relationships is Giving Voice (giving-voice.org). It convenes online forums and periodic national and regional gatherings.

I propose that these facts give us a glimpse of God's dream. Martin Luther King, Jr.'s, famous "I Have a Dream" speech laid out a future that few of his contemporaries could imagine, but which, once articulated, found resonance with many more and was a source of the godly energy needed to make the dream a reality. I suggest that God, too, has a dream. God's dream for religious life in the United States is a dream bigger than those of us who are living the life right now, a dream bigger than any of our congregations, individually or collectively, a dream the size of God, "more than we can all ask or imagine" (Eph 3:20). I believe this dream centers around some important elements: charism, community, and connectivity.

Charism is the deep story of each of our congregations, the story of what was done and the more important story of why it was done and why it was done in a particular way. We, as members of the minority cohorts of our various communities, are in a position to hear the stories, to breathe in this spirit, and to live the spirituality of the institutes. We gather the riches of each of our congregations as they nurture the life while the new is emerging and unfolding. We integrate the "DNA" of the charisms so that we can carry these charisms forward, blessing those who have shared it with us so generously.

Community is an imperative element of the dream, a sign of our times. Individuals, families, and whole societies are feeling the fragmentation of modern living, and many spiritual thinkers and writers are telling us that healing our personal and global spirits will happen through community—or it will not happen at all.

Connectivity is the final element of the dream. We will not build institutions, but webs, not mega-communities, but mini-communities in relationship. Not mastery, but ministry. So many of the most influential movements in the new consciousness are small organizations that are self-organizing and networked. This is the genius of the Occupy movement, of the peace movement, and of the Arab spring.

The fourth chapter begins the task of reimagining the elements of religious life. In this task, the minority reaches instinctively for the tools of group discernment rather than those of strategic planning. We will gather in living rooms rather than conference rooms; we will use Skype and social media rather than study groups and five-year plans.

The first task is to reimagine the vows as life-enhancing covenants that seek to incarnate the beatitudes here and now. The vow of poverty invites us to create an alternate economy of simplicity of life and interdependence in community, and in solidarity with the poor and marginalized, a gift economy. It is not an option but a necessity if we are to form communities where we are radically committed to living the beatitudes. We reimagine the vow of celibate chastity as a freedom for relationship both in community and in ministry. Our primary life commitment within the community frees us to model reconciling love. Our vow of obedience enables us to create an alternate political system based not on power but on love and service. We are called to listen to one another and to build a humane lifestyle that resists the frenetic will to action and will to power. We acknowledge that we are not the saviors of the world, but that our prophetic witness to gospel living is our greatest contribution to the in-breaking of the spirit of the beatitudes in our world. It is important that we make these commitments for life, because this lifetime commitment affects the quality of our being together. This does not exclude the possibility of other forms of commitment lived in complementarity to the permanent vowed commitment.

We reimagine community as a privileged place where we can take seriously a commitment of living the beatitudes very deliberately and integrating them into the life of the community. We commit to living simply and sustainably and living lightly on the earth. We share our goods and live in reconciliation. We will choose to locate our communities in areas abandoned by the "empire," those areas neglected by the holders of power, perhaps economically depressed areas or rural areas. From these places we will commit to systematically "deconstructing" the "-isms" that hold others and ourselves in subjugation: racism, sexism, consumerism, and so on. The quality of this community will affect our lives, our spirituality, and our ministry to those in need.

We reimagine mission. Many of our communities were founded in a time when only religious could commit themselves to a life of ministry. Family commitments and gender stereotypes excluded people, particularly women, from lives of service. However, today it is commonplace for men and women to commit to ministry and to a life of service, not only within church settings, but in the wider nonprofit sector; they may serve as social entrepreneurs. Thus we will have to reimagine the place of ministry in this world.

Community itself will be a part of the mission of religious life in the future. The commitment to faith-based intentional community affects not only those who live it but those who live around it and share in various ways in the life of the community. At the same time we are likely to make deliberate choices to take on some form of ministry as a community, even as we continue to seek ministry outside the local community, to advance gospel values, and to assist with the sustenance of the group. We may rehab the community living space or create a community garden where we grow some of our own food. Members of the local community may decide to become involved in a particular nonprofit or parish project. We may make a commitment to share in the work of one of the ministries in which one of the community members works. This would not be added to the top of an already hectic schedule but something that the group integrates into its commitment to balanced living.

As a group we will also want to discern collectively when and how we can free one or more members to work at the margins, serving those who cannot otherwise be helped. Mission will also support community by ensuring our solidarity with the working poor and being an expression of our commitment to justice, spirituality, and sustainability.

The fifth chapter turns to practicalities of governance and formation for the emerging reality. The emerging life form will not need the infrastructure that has served the dominant cohort. That infrastructure was built for thousands of sisters staffing large institutional ministries. These ministries are now in the hands of capable and committed lay people. Emerging religious life will have the task of imagining the infrastructure that will support and enhance its life. Likewise, it will have the task of reimagining formation. We will explore how newer members can be welcomed and integrated to this new life form that is smaller, more local, and more autonomous.

CONCLUSION

The reality of the religious life, the church from which it springs, and contemporary society all point to the emergence of a new form of religious life. Those in and around religious life have known for decades that something new was coming, and we have strained "the eyes of our hearts" to catch a glimpse of what it might look like. We knew that this new development was beyond our imagination, but when it finally appeared, it would do honor to the heritage of religious life. The day is finally dawning, and the new form is beginning to emerge in our spirits, imaginations, and conversations. The reinvention of religious life for today calls for a renewed commitment to the choice of radical Christianity that inspired, attracted, and sustained religious communities of every age. We are discovering anew how to live the beatitudes in a deliberate way. We take inspiration from the

New Monasticism movement, which has sought to commit to these same values in the evangelical context. The twelve marks of New Monasticism, discussed in Chapter 4, are a good point of departure in imagining the life we hope to live. In this way we can be a blessing to those who have come before us in religious life, and to those who follow, as well as for the wider Christian community and the world at large.

CHAPTER ONE

THE HISTORY OF RELIGIOUS LIFE FROM AN EVOLUTIONARY PERSPECTIVE

With a view toward understanding what is emerging, this chapter explores the development of major movements in the two-thousand-year history of religious life and traces how these movements brought us to the present moment in the church. We examine this history from the viewpoint of today's shifting consciousness. Inspired by Vatican II, the renewal of religious life in the second half of the twentieth century was a major movement in the contemporary history of religious life. However, this did not mark the end of the story; instead, it prepared us for a more fundamental reinvention of the life that will bring us into the middle of the twenty-first century. Historically, religious life has reinvented itself every five hundred years or so, with the new forms continuing to exist alongside the old.

DESERT MOVEMENT

In the early Christian centuries, desert hermits, virgins, and pilgrims sought to embrace a life of deep personal commitment to prayer and gospel living, to the exclusion of any other primary life commitment. We have writings from these fathers and mothers of the desert, who heard the call to a more radical form of life.

According to Western tradition, religious life as we know it today traces its origins back to the ascetics of the Egyptian Desert starting early in the third century. Eastern Christianity however traces the origins of religious life right back to apostolic times, and understands the continuous presence of ascetics, hermits and monastics through the ages to be a form of apostolic succession alongside that of the clergy and bishops.[1]

In the earliest days, the bond between a community and its members was seen as a practical means of mutual support and of initiation of new monks and nuns. Cenobitic or communitarian monasticism existed alongside eremetic forms, in which hermits lived in greater solitude. These were seen as two ways of living out the basic monastic lifestyle, which itself was simply a more intense response to the call of the gospel. In addition to these more stable forms of monastic life, there is also an ancient tradition of pilgrimage, which was described by Gregory of Nyssa, Jerome, and Egeria;[2] in early Christian times these pilgrimages could last for many months, or even years.[3] These pilgrims left the security of family and homeland, relying on God and on the kindness of strangers as they made their way to holy places and witnessed to the gospel wherever they went. As the geographical journey unfolded, the pilgrim was also making a spiritual journey. *The Way of a Pilgrim* is a more recent text that follows in this tradition. It describes the pilgrimage of an eighteenth-century Russian monk who set out

---

[1] Boniface Luykx, *Eastern Monasticism and the Future of the Church* (Redwood Valley, CA: Holy Transfiguration Monastery, 1993), 93ff.

[2] Philip Schaff, ed., *Nicene and Post-Nicene Christianity: A.D. 311–600* (New York: Charles Scribner, 1889), 584; idem, *A Select Library of the Nicene and Post-Nicene Fathers of the Christian Church*, vol. 6, *Nicene and Post-Nicene Fathers II* (Edinburgh: T&T Clark, 1886), xxxiiiff; Egeria, *Egeria: Diary of a Pilgrimage*, ed. George E. Gingras (New York: Newman Press, 1970).

[3] Simon Coleman and John Elsner, *Pilgrimage: Past and Present in the World Religions* (Cambridge, MA: Harvard University Press, 1995), 16.

to learn the ways of prayer, and gradually learns the path of the Jesus Prayer. The book begins:

> By the grace of God I am a Christian, by my deeds a great sinner, and by my calling a homeless wanderer of humblest origin, roaming from place to place. My possessions consist of a knapsack with dry crusts of bread on my back and in my bosom the Holy Bible. That is all.[4]

A feature of these early forms of religious life was the individual commitment to a solitary life of prayer, penance, and spiritual practice. Sometimes the individuals made vows to practice a certain asceticism, for example, vows of celibacy, or a vow to make a pilgrimage. Many witnessed to great holiness of life, but some embraced severe forms of asceticism that at times could be considered bizarre.

Nevertheless, there were many very holy and revered desert fathers and mothers who sought to develop a sound spiritual practice. They lived simple lives of prayer. Some gained a reputation for spiritual counsel, and people from towns and villages sought out their wisdom and recorded their sayings in books that are still available today.

Anthony of the Desert is one of the most famous examples of this type of religious life. His story was recorded by Saint Athanasius and from this we can learn some of the basic elements of this way of life. Anthony led an unremarkable Christian life until he received a special call or invitation by God to a life of deeper prayer and more authentic gospel living. He heard the words of the Gospel of Matthew: "Go, sell what you own, and give the money to the poor, and you will have treasure in heaven; then come, follow me" (Mk 10:21). Taking these words literally, he sold all his earthly goods and gave away the proceeds, after first providing for his family. Then he went to an isolated place on the edge of town and sought to live a life of

---

[4] Helen Bacovcin, trans., *The Way of a Pilgrim and The Pilgrim Continues His Way* (New York: Image Books, 1992), 3.

prayer and penance, escaping from the cares and concerns of everyday life in order to seek the Divine. Athanasius recounts a tale of extreme fasting and temptation by the forces of evil. In this quest Anthony originally sought advice from a more experienced hermit, but later he retired to an isolated cave to work out his way of salvation in solitude, penance, and prayer.

In time, Anthony achieved a certain balance in life and gained a reputation for holiness and for the sound spiritual advice that he gave to those who sought out his wisdom. Gradually, he retreated further into the wilderness to live a more solitary life, but due to his reputation, followers continued to seek him out. Many came to follow his example of a simple life of prayer and contemplation. He imparted the practical wisdom that he had obtained from his years of spiritual practice, teaching his followers to live a life of prayer and solitude accompanied by simple manual work. He wove baskets as he prayed, finding the simple work to be an apt tool to still the mind and focus his heart in prayer. Anthony did not establish a community or an organizational structure for his followers but simply imparted advice and showed them the way by the example of his own life.

Eastern Christianity has always focused more than the West on the mystical nature of the gospel message and on the benefits of asceticism in leading the person into a deeper spirituality. It finds examples for this practice in the Hebrew prophets, John the Baptist, and Jesus himself. From these examples early hermits took their cues, going into the wilderness to pray and fast and do battle with the powers of evil. In addition to the story of Anthony, early Christian literature evidences individuals who embraced lives of celibacy and penance for the sake of the kingdom of heaven. Hermits, virgins, widows, and pilgrims committed themselves to lives of holiness, often seeking solitude within or on the outskirts of towns, or even deep in the wilderness and desert. Though most lived alone, there is also evidence of groups and even fairly large communities or monasteries in the desert.[5]

---

[5] Luc Brésard, *A History of Monastic Spirituality* (Scourmont, Belgium: Scourmont Abbey, n.d.), scourmont.be website.

These communities organized their labor, held all their goods in common, and replaced the more extreme forms of asceticism with orderly lives of prayer and work in community.

It is unknown how many individuals followed this early form of religious life, but there are countless records of individuals and some groups who lived lives of exceptional holiness and left stories and sayings that continue to inspire Christians today. It is also known that not all who set out to live this lifestyle were able to lead lives of exemplary holiness. By the fifth century wandering ascetics had gained a reputation for being unruly and disruptive.[6] The monastic movement arose partially in response to this reality.

MONASTICISM

Religious life found new expression in monastic communities in the fifth century. By gathering in communities, Christians found support and challenge for living their radical commitment to prayer and gospel living. Augustine and Benedict wrote rules that survive to this day and continue to inspire communities. Their rules were not intended to found the orders that would eventually bear their names. Instead, they set out to provide practical advice to the communities that had gathered around them.

Augustine

Saint Augustine (354–430), after completing his studies, lived a dissolute life and worked as an academic. He found himself attracted by the teachings of Christianity long before he actually converted. The story of his spiritual journey is found in his *Confessions*, one of the greatest spiritual classics of all times. There he recounts the story of his conversion:

---

[6] Benedict Verheyen, *The Holy Rule of St. Benedict* (Atchison, KS: St. Benedict's Abbey, 1949), chap. 1.

I flung myself down under a fig tree—how I know not—and gave free course to my tears. The streams of my eyes gushed out an acceptable sacrifice to thee. And, not indeed in these words, but to this effect, I cried to thee: "And thou, O Lord, how long? How long, O Lord? Wilt thou be angry forever? Oh, remember not against us our former iniquities." For I felt that I was still enthralled by them. I sent up these sorrowful cries: "How long, how long? Tomorrow and tomorrow? Why not now? Why not this very hour make an end to my uncleanness?"

I was saying these things and weeping in the most bitter contrition of my heart, when suddenly I heard the voice of a boy or a girl I know not which—coming from the neighboring house, chanting over and over again, "Pick it up, read it; pick it up, read it." . . . So I quickly returned to the bench where Alypius was sitting, for there I had put down the apostle's book when I had left there. I snatched it up, opened it, and in silence read the paragraph on which my eyes first fell: "Not in rioting and drunkenness, not in chambering and wantonness, not in strife and envying, but put on the Lord Jesus Christ, and make no provision for the flesh to fulfill the lusts thereof." I wanted to read no further, nor did I need to. For instantly, as the sentence ended, there was infused in my heart something like the light of full certainty and all the gloom of doubt vanished away.[7]

This moment was a turning point that led Augustine to give his life over to Christianity. Some time after his conversion Augustine returned to his family home with some companions; together they began living a monastic lifestyle. Although he was a prolific writer and wrote extensively on many aspects of Christian life and community, Augustine did not intend to write a rule for the group. However, he did write a letter to a

---

[7] *Confessions of St. Augustine*, trans. E. B. Pusey (New York: Arden Library, 1982), 8.12.

community of women that seemed to be experiencing some difficulties. The letter, comprising fewer than five thousand words, came to be regarded as the Augustinian rule, and its influence extends beyond the Augustinian order to countless religious orders and congregations that base their way of life on it.

Benedict

Saint Benedict (480–543) was born in Nursia in central Italy. Though he probably did not intend to found a religious order, he did establish several communities of monks in central and southern Italy and wrote a rule for monasteries based on the earlier religious life but brought to it a sense of balance and moderation, an instinct for the value of community, and an understanding of some of the fundamentals of good community building.

Before completing his studies, Benedict sought a secluded life with a view to rejecting the dissolute life of some of his fellow students. He soon became a hermit and was guided by a monk from a nearby monastery. After some years monks from another monastery sought him to be their abbot, and Benedict reluctantly consented. Before long, this arrangement soured, and the monks tried to poison him. Benedict was miraculously delivered and left the place. His reputation grew, and he founded twelve monasteries in the region, each with twelve monks and a leader. Benedict held a position of honor over the entire group.

Benedict wrote his rule to guide the life of these monasteries. It consists of seventy-three short chapters, some consisting of just a few sentences. The guidance it gives falls in two categories: on the one hand, he invites his followers to live a gospel-centered life; and on the other, he gives guidance on orderly community living. He urges everyone to live a life of humility and obedience, gentleness, and discernment. Acknowledging the human condition, he also provides guidelines for situations in which a member of the community is not living up to this ideal. He describes in detail the prescriptions for community prayer, called the work of God, or *opus Dei*. Finally, he outlines the governance of the monastery.

Significance of Monasticism

Monasticism has been credited with saving Western civilization after the fall of the Roman Empire led to a "dark night" in the history of European civilization.[8] It certainly played an important role in preserving Christianity in the Western Church and in preserving the great works of civilization and culture for future generations. Men and women gathered in monasteries, inspired by gospel ideals, and committed to living sober, balanced lives of prayer and work. They were guided in this by Benedict's rule, which he himself describes as an outline for beginners.[9] It has offered sound advice on the path to holiness to generation after generation of monastics as well as to seekers from every walk of life.

As the centuries passed, monasteries became centers of spirituality, learning, and culture. They also amassed great wealth and became major players in the politics of medieval Europe. With wealth and power came corruption and intrigue, which hindered the spiritual growth of the monasteries and prompted reform movements within monasticism itself. In addition, by the Middle Ages the church and society had changed drastically, and the scene was set for the emergence of new forms of religious life brought by Dominic and Francis and their followers.[10]

MENDICANTS

In the Middle Ages religious life reinvented itself as some of the large and powerful monasteries found it difficult to maintain

---

[8] Benedict XVI, "Saint Benedict of Norcia" (homily presented at the General Audience, Rome, April 9, 2008).

[9] Verheyen, "The Holy Rule of St. Benedict," chap. 73.

[10] Maria Casey, "The Evolution of New Forms of Consecrated Life," *Studia Canonica* 36 (2002): 463–86.

their fidelity to monasticism's founding ideals. The mendicants sought lives of poverty and simplicity. Franciscans and Dominicans are prime examples of this life form.

> Laxity and growing wealth in monasteries as well as a shift from a land-based to a money-based commerce along with growth in urban centers, favored new developments.[11]

Francis

Saint Francis (1182–1226) was the son of a wealthy Italian merchant. Enjoying all the privileges of his class, Francis was a high-spirited youth and served for a time as a soldier. He was taken prisoner, became ill in prison, and was later ransomed by his father.[12] During his convalescence, he had a conversion experience, broke with his family, and turned to a life of simplicity. As Francis's spirituality grew, he sought a life of solitude and prayed in deserted places, embracing "holy poverty." Once, in the Church of San Damiano, while immersed in prayer, he heard the voice of Christ calling him to "rebuild my church." He began to rebuild the church building of San Damiano but soon came to realize that it was not just the building that needed his ministrations, but the entire people of God. In time, Francis came to realize that his call was not that of a lonely hermit but one of service to the wider community.

> Then with great fervor of spirit and joy of mind he began to preach repentance to all, with simple words but largeness of heart edifying his hearers. For his word was like a blazing fire piercing through the inmost heart, and it filled the minds of all with wonder.[13]

---

[11] Ibid., 473.

[12] Thomas of Celano, *The First Life of St. Francis of Assisi* (Marion, IN: Triangle, 2000), part 1, chap. 1.

[13] Ibid., chap. 10.

Francis gathered followers in the town of Assisi, and his followers are now found in all parts of the globe. His spirituality is based on his love of God, whom he experienced in all creation. In addition, he established a form of religious life that responded to the evolving needs of church and society.

Clare

Saint Clare of Assisi (1194–1253), inspired by the same gospel imperative as Francis, joined Francis at San Damiano despite her family's objections. She was joined by her sister Agnes and other women to form communities in the area. In that period it was not acceptable for women to go about preaching as the Franciscan men did. Instead, the women lived in communities and sought to live a radically austere lifestyle marked by poverty and penance. Francis gave Clare and her companions a form of life, a rule adapting the practice of the brothers to the women's community.[14] The Fourth Lateran Council (1215) required all religious orders to adopt an existing rule;[15] Clare and her community were required to adopt the rule of Saint Benedict.[16] Nonetheless, Clare continued to maintain her conviction that she and Francis had a very distinct way of life. She continued to live the life and work with ecclesiastical authorities to obtain approval of her way of life. In the end, Clare wrote her own rule, which was finally accepted by the pope when she was dying. This was the first rule written by a woman in which

> Clare expresses the initial inspiration of her way of life and, at the same time, acknowledges that the forms of life

---

[14] Clare of Assisi, "Testament," in *Clare of Assisi—The Lady: Early Documents*, ed. Regis Armstrong (New York: New York City Press, 2006), 60–65.

[15] Norman P. Tanner and Giuseppe Alberigo, *Decrees of the Ecumenical Councils* (Washington DC: Georgetown University Press, 1990), Lateran IV, Constitution 13.

[16] Aidan McGrath, "Between Charism and Institution: The Approval of the Rule of Saint Clare in 1253," *Studia Canonica* 31 (1997): 434.

given to her by ecclesiastical authority have proved useful in regulating certain matters of a practical nature.[17]

Like many founders and foundresses of religious institutes, Clare had to cling to the ideal for gospel living that was her unique inspiration and gift to the church. At the same time she had to live within the culture of her day, both in civil society and in the church. Commenting on Clare's lifelong struggle to have her way of life accepted, Aidan McGrath states:

> Founders and foundresses were not and are not comfortable people to deal with; theirs has been the prophetic role, the call to challenge the status quo and point to something different within the life of the Church, local or universal. A person like Clare would probably have inspired fear and dread in the hearts of many working in the Curia of her day. Yet we must remember that she, like countless others, was driven by a special grace from God, a grace that had to be discerned over a long number of years.[18]

Dominic

Saint Dominic (1170–1221) was born in the village of Caleruega in the kingdom of Castile, Spain. He began as a diocesan cleric in the cathedral of the Diocese of Osma in what is now northern Spain. In the course of his work he traveled into southern France, and he discovered there a great spiritual hunger among the people he encountered. Clergy of the day were generally poorly educated and many, both priests and bishops, lived lives of luxury that were a scandal to the people. Caught up in the machinations of power, monasteries and bishops vied with kings and emperors for wealth and prestige, leaving the spiritual care of the people in a poor state.[19] Like Francis, Dominic sought to

---

[17] Ibid., 442.

[18] Ibid., 447–48.

[19] Jean Guiraud, *Saint Dominic* (London: Duckworth, 1913), 16–19, archive. org/details/saintdominic00guirrich.

respond to the needs of church and society in his day. He was able to see that the current structures of religious life no longer served the needs of the growing urban centers. Instead, a new type of religious life was needed that would bring the dedication and education found within traditional monasteries out into the communities to address the spiritual needs of the people. Living the gospel and proclaiming it to those in need would require a more flexible organizational structure.

After returning from his journey, Dominic gathered a group of men who shared his dream. Even though the Fourth Lateran Council (1215) forbade the establishment of new orders or writing of new rules,[20] Dominic received official approval of his rule in 1216.[21]

Significance of the Mendicants

The Dominican clerics and the lay Franciscans brought fresh energy into religious life through their innovations. They were inspired by the same evangelical radicalism that had led ascetics into the Egyptian desert and called men and women down through the centuries to embrace monastic life. Yet in the new situation in which they found themselves, they realized that religious life would be more effective if members had the freedom to move from house to house. For Francis, poverty held the key, and around it he built his rule and his order. For Dominic, preaching lay at the heart of the call. But for both founders the autonomy of the individual monasteries in the Benedictine tradition was problematic. That autonomy allowed monasteries the freedom to govern their own affairs, but it did not provide a mechanism of regular renewal. Franciscans and Dominicans were centralized, allowing for regular interchange among communities

---

[20] Tanner and Alberigo, *Decrees of the Ecumenical Councils*, Lateran IV, Constitution 13.

[21] Honorius III, "Religiosam Vitam," in *Saint Dominique: L'idée, L'homme Et L'oeuvre*, by Pierre Mandonnet and M. H. Vicaire, vol. 1 (Paris: Desclée de Brouwer, 1938), 54–59.

and providing a means of recalling members to the ideals on which the communities were founded.

At the end of the thirteenth century, which saw the foundation of the great Franciscan and Dominican families, Pope Boniface VIII promulgated the Apostolic Constitution Periculoso.[22] This decree mandated the complete enclosure of women religious; once a woman made profession in religious life, she could not leave the monastery at all, an exception being made if the monastery were on fire. The cloistering of women religious has had a deep and lasting effect on women's religious life. The decree of Boniface was reinforced some centuries later at the Council of Trent.[23] Although it was variously enforced, it is difficult to overestimate the significance of the strict cloister, which mandated nearly complete isolation of the entire movement of women's religious life from the wider cultural context for almost six centuries, from 1298 to 1983. Over the centuries many women religious continually sought ways to engage in ministry outside the cloister and were able to do this, but only with strict limitations on their activities, dress, and interactions.

APOSTOLIC ORDERS

In the sixteenth century the apostolic orders arose in response to the pressing needs of the church and of society. The Jesuits, the Sisters of St. Joseph, and many other religious orders and congregations arose to carry out the mission of Jesus in the world around them. It is important to examine this form of life in some detail, both with respect to the innovation that it

---

[22] Boniface VIII, *Apostolic Constitution Periculoso*, 1298, in Elizabeth M. Makowski, *Canon Law and Cloistered Women: Periculoso and Its Commentators, 1298–1545*, Studies in Medieval and Early Modern Canon Law (Washington DC: Catholic University of America Press, 1997).

[23] Council of Trent, *Decree on Regulars and Nuns*, November 25, 1551, in J. Waterworth, *The Canons and Decrees of the Sacred and Oecumenical Council of Trent* (London: Dolman, 1848), 1563.

brought to the life and the way in which it interacted with the wider society.

Ignatius Loyola

In 1534, Ignatius Loyola (1491–1556) founded the Society of Jesus, an order of secular clergy who committed themselves to the reform of the church and the evangelization of the "pagans" in the newly discovered continents. In the history of spirituality Ignatius and his order introduced some remarkable renewals. The personal spirituality of Ignatius and his own process of conversion is reflected in the *Spiritual Exercises,* a manual for a four-week retreat that he drew up for his order. Ignatian spirituality was a spirituality of service, oriented to action in the world. The Jesuits considered their work as a mission to serve the world; they were available at every place where their service was needed. Their spirituality was a world-affirming spirituality, which was expressed in a positive appreciation of human values and was connected to action. Formally, the Jesuits contributed to the renewal of Catholic spirituality by introducing new methods that influenced the personal development of the spiritual life: periodic retreats with precise instructions and methods; spiritual guidance; and the establishment of confraternities in every Jesuit institution. In the course of the sixteenth century two currents originated in the spirituality of Spanish Jesuits, one more ascetic, the other more mystically oriented. The balance between the two was preserved by Jerónimo Nadal (1507–80), "the theologian of Ignatian spirituality," who summarized the spiritual ideal of the Jesuits in the phrase "in actione contemplativus" (contemplative in action).[24]

An Apostolic Foundation of Women

We will take a little more time to set the stage for the foundation of a group of apostolic women religious. As with each of the

---

[24] Leo Kenis, "History of Religious Life—Spirituality in the Seventeenth and Eighteenth Centuries," lecture notes (Leuven, Belgium, 2009), 23.

preceding forms of religious life, the founders and foundresses were responding to the particular social and religious context in which they lived. In viewing the history of religious life with a view to understanding its evolution, it is important to see not only what each group did, but to see why it did it. What were the particular socio-political and religious forces at work in its time and place? How did the founding generation respond to these forces? How was it shaped by them and how did it resist these pressures? Important lessons for the future of religious life can be teased out by a nuanced understanding of the particular context in which the founding generation lived and by understanding the interplay between the founding inspiration and its context.

Socio-Political Situation

Seventeenth-century France was a time of political, cultural, social, and religious unrest. The preceding century had been dominated by wars of religion primarily fought between French Catholics and Protestant Huguenots. The Edict of Nantes sought to end the conflict by providing a measure of tolerance and some political freedoms to the Huguenots. However, the edict did not put an end to hostilities between the factions. Political tensions elsewhere in Europe only contributed to the dissension.[25] "It was that hinge time . . . a time of violence motivated especially by religious intolerance."[26]

The Thirty Years War (1618–48) began in Prague and soon ensnared most of Europe in a conflict that divided along religious lines.

> In this constellation, the later involvement of France in the war was crucial: France sided with the Protestants—although it was predominantly Catholic (but also Gallicanist). The causes of the war were multiple: economic,

---

[25] Ibid., 11.

[26] Wendy M. Wright, ed., *Francis De Sales, Jane De Chantal: Letters of Spiritual Direction* (Mahwah, NJ: Paulist Press, 1988), 18.

political, cultural. However, people did not conceive these underlying factors as causes of war: for the popular mind, religious issues were at stake.[27]

Though France recovered more quickly than other countries, the years of conflict left significant marks on the people. There was a general feeling of frustration and uncertainty. The people came to realize that with the loss of religious unity, Europe lost an important mediator of rival interests. With the rise of Protestantism, the pope could no longer effectively arbitrate between warring rulers. In addition, there arose a general skepticism toward traditional authority and sources of truth. Along with this unrest and questioning of authority came an effort to return to the sources of Christianity and culture.[28]

The Ecclesial Context
The Catholic Church was also very much in disarray in the seventeenth century. Most clergy lacked even minimal spiritual and intellectual formation, leading to all manner of abuses. Monasteries were populated by individuals placed there by their families without a thought to vocation or spirituality. This led to mediocrity and abuses in the monastic life. The bishop's office was a privilege of the nobility and often was seen as a position of power and prestige to be acquired and disposed of for personal and family gain. Individual Catholics without support from the church were left to find their own way to God. Nor did the social or political state of affairs offer much in the way of stability or direction. The Council of Trent (1563) had attempted reform, with decrees addressing clerical conduct and formation, the office of bishop, and the life of monasteries. Initially, these decrees were widely ignored.[29]

---

[27] Kenis, "History of Religious Life," 8.

[28] Ted A. Campbell, *The Religion of the Heart: A Study of European Religious Life in the Seventeenth and Eighteenth Centuries* (Columbia: University of South Carolina Press, 1991), 11.

[29] Kenis, "History of Religious Life," 10.

A significant impetus for change came from charismatic religious leaders who began reform movements in southern Europe that began to have effect toward the end of the sixteenth century. Ignatius Loyola (1491–1556), Teresa of Avila (1515–82), and John of the Cross (1542–91) expounded a fundamental renewal of spirituality, focusing on the personal and subjective interiorization of the spiritual life. They sought to improve the spiritual lives of individuals, both within their religious orders and beyond. Though their efforts were not without opposition, their teachings and their followers made significant contributions to the spirituality of the period and continue to influence the church today.[30]

This opened the way for an abundant flowering of spirituality in seventeenth-century France and the development of an approach that has been called religion of the heart. This was characterized by a new sense of sacramentality that viewed the sacred and profane not as separate realms, but as profoundly united. It also saw a rise of a rigorous personal asceticism aimed at purifying individuals and preparing them for a personal encounter with the Divine. Characteristic of this approach was a strong sense of popular piety that tapped into the emotions.

> At the turn of the sixteenth to the seventeenth century, in France a number of religious and spiritual movements came to the fore, which exercised a decisive role in the spectacular spiritual renewal of catholic life. They made the seventeenth century in France (the 'Grand Siècle') the 'siècle des saints.'[31]

These movements deserve special attention because they form the context for the foundation of many new religious orders.

The *milieux dévots* attempted to combine the reformation of the French church with a spiritual revival. An important

---

[30] Ibid.
[31] Ibid., 13.

example was Marie de l'Incarnation (1566–1618), who began to live a life of spirituality and charity to the poor and to receive people in her home in the waning years of the sixteenth century. Benoît de Canfield helped to guide this movement and presented the ultimate stage of the spiritual life as the prayer in which a person transcends all conceptual and discursive stages and reaches a state of *anéantissement* (annihilation) of the human will in the Divine. In this way the person reaches a state of stable union with God, even in this life.[32]

Another movement was that of the confraternities, which promoted popular devotion among the people in local regions and groupings. Many of these confraternities were devoted to the Blessed Sacrament, the Sacred Heart, or the Blessed Virgin Mary. They might be established in a parish, professional guild, or other social gathering of people. These groups sometimes aroused ecclesiastical suspicion if they seemed to be beyond clerical control. For this reason some became hidden or secret societies to avoid official scrutiny.[33]

Francis de Sales (1567–1622) had a great influence in this period. Bishop of Geneva from 1602 through 1622, he "led the entire century into the world of devotion and the love of God."[34] De Sales sought to teach a way of holiness that was attractive and accessible to the common people, saying, "It's a mistake, even a heresy, to want to banish the devout life from the soldier's camp, the manual worker's workshop, the court of princes, the homes of married people."[35] He also taught the importance of surrender to God, *remise en Dieu*, a surrender that is available to all persons: "No sooner does a man take the trouble to give

---

[32] Ibid., 17.

[33] Ibid., 13.

[34] Michael J. Buckley, "Seventeenth-Century French Spirituality: Three Figures," in *Christian Spirituality: Post-Reformation and Modern*, ed. Louis Dupré, Don E. Saliers, and John Meyendorf, World Spirituality (New York: Crossroad, 1991), 32.

[35] Francis de Sales, *Introduction to the Devout Life* (New York: Vintage, 2002), 8.

even a little thought to the godhead than his heart thrills with pleasure."[36]

De Sales also emphasized the gentleness of God, who "governs with an incomparable sweetness, for love has no convicts nor slaves, but brings all things under its obedience with a force so delightful, that as nothing is so strong as love nothing also is so sweet as its strength."[37] In 1610, De Sales, together with Jane Frances de Chantal, founded the Order of the Visitation of Holy Mary, or the Visitation Sisters. Their intent was to gather women who would not be subject to the rules of cloister and other austerities but instead would be able to dedicate themselves to works of charity. Although some of the austerities were mitigated and works of charity were embraced, within a few short years cloister was accepted in response to the prevailing practice for women's religious orders and the requirements of the Council of Trent's *Decree on Regulars and Nuns*. "Gentleness toward neighbor" characterized the spirit of the Visitation and this gentle, lenient approach, with attention for beauty and goodness, appealed to many.[38]

Foundation of the Sisters of St. Joseph in Le Puy, France

In 1646, a group of women gathered in Le Puy in southern France. The women and their Jesuit guide sought to respond to the pressing religious, social, and cultural needs of their day. This could not be done by women who remained in cloisters. For this reason the group did not intend to become a religious order but rather a group of lay women serving the needs of the neighborhoods. The early documents indicate that this group of women was to be a secret society, a "Little Design," like a pattern in a piece of lace.[39] This pattern could be repeated over

---

[36] Francis de Sales, *Treatise on the Love of God*, trans. Henry Benedict Mackey (New York: Benziger Brothers, 1884), 37.

[37] Ibid.

[38] Kenis, "History of Religious Life," 21.

[39] Marguerite Vacher, *Des "Regulieres" Dans Le Siecle: Les Soeurs De Saint-Joseph Du Pere Medaille Aux XVIIe Et XVIIIe Siecles* (Saltillo, Mexico: Adosa, 1991), 147.

and over, making a splendid impression, though each pattern seems insignificant. Likewise, the small communities of women would live and work in simplicity and service. They addressed the pressing needs of the day by a return to the gospel sources and seeking to incarnate the gospel in their time and place. In doing this they did not see the need to take on the structural elements that had become integral to women's religious life, namely, strict cloister, prescribed prayers, and a particular style of dress. The women did choose to wear widows' garb, which allowed them to move about freely in service of their mission, because other women were not permitted to go about the city without a male companion. Little is known about this group of women, who were soon disbanded, though their existence is alluded to in the subsequent stories of the foundation of the Sisters of St. Joseph.

In 1650, the Sisters of St. Joseph were founded in Le Puy by six women with the assistance of the Jesuit Jean-Paul Médaille, and they were accepted by the bishop, Mgr. de Maupas, on October 15, 1650. On March 10, 1651, Bishop Henri de Maupas granted ecclesiastical approval to these women.[40] Of the six women who became the first six Sisters of St. Joseph, only one, a widow, could sign her name, and only two brought any kind of financial dowry. The group immediately took on the administration of the hospital-orphanage in the rue de Montferrand in Le Puy.[41]

The following year another house of Sisters of St. Joseph was established in Merlhes, a nearby town, and each succeeding year saw the foundation of one or two new houses of Sisters of St. Joseph until the region was dotted with communities.[42] Each

[40] Letter of Bishop Henry de Maupas of Puy for the Establishment of the Sisters of St. Joseph. Reprinted in "Constitutions of the Congregation of the Sisters of St. Joseph" (St. Louis, MO: Wm. J. Mullin, 1847), 183–84.

[41] Mary McGlone, *Communidad Para El Mundo: La Historia De Las Hermanas De San José De Carondelet* (Lima, Perú: Hermanas de San José, 2009), 44.

[42] Vacher, *Des "Regulieres" Dans Le Siecle*, 451.

house enjoyed a good measure of autonomy, which allowed the group to grow and develop organically and to respond to the needs of its region without constant reference to some central authority. The constitution was first printed in 1694 in Vienne, France, but by this time there were already several manuscript editions with significant differences among them. Once the Vienne edition was printed, it became the standard and gradually supplanted other editions.[43]

By the time of the French Revolution, the group had spread through twelve dioceses in southeastern France but still had little central authority. Although most of the houses were disbanded during the revolution, because of its decentralized structure many of the groups survived and were able to reorganize after the hostilities subsided. In 1807, Mother St. John Fontbonne, who had narrowly escaped death by the guillotine, gathered the Sisters of St. Joseph who had been disbanded and women from other religious institutes. At the invitation of the bishop she moved to Lyon, and from there she oversaw the reestablishment of the congregation and its expansion to many parts of France and beyond.[44] "Between 1806 and 1816 Mother St. John brought together at Lyon sisters from at least twenty-eight communities which had existed before the conflagration."[45]

Due to her historical situation Mother St. John saw the need for a more centralized governance structure. This structure required a change in the constitutions, which was approved in 1874.[46] In addition to the growing congregation with a motherhouse at Lyon, several groups of Sisters of St. Joseph severed ties

---

[43] Ibid., 177.

[44] Abbé (Jean-Joseph) Rivaux, *Life of Rev. Mother St. John Fontbonne, Foundress and First Superior-General of the Congregation of the Sisters of St. Joseph in Lyons* (Charleston, SC: Nabu Press, 2011).

[45] French Federation of the Sisters of St. Joseph, *Vital Roots—Powerful Witness: Stories from the July 1994 Bulletin of the French Federation*, trans. Francis Cecilia English, *Letting in Joy by Looking to Our Past* (Rochester, NY: Sisters of St. Joseph of Rochester, 1996), 33.

[46] Rivaux, *Life of Rev. Mother St. John Fontbonne,* 74.

with Lyon and established themselves as separate congregations with either diocesan or papal approval.[47]

Institutionalization of the Life

Like so many other apostolic communities of women religious, the Sisters of St. Joseph experienced rapid growth and increasing institutionalization of their life and ministry. In the seventeenth century the sisters had lived in small local communities and operated somewhat autonomously, following a common rule, but adapting to local needs and circumstances. As the group expanded, there was a need to centralize and standardize. New members came to centralized novitiates to receive their initial formation, to study the life, and to learn the practices of their community. From that central location they could be sent to a growing number of schools, hospitals, and other facilities that were built and run by the sisters. As the groups grew and expanded over the nineteenth and first half of the twentieth centuries, the life became more standardized.

In 1940, Rome's Sacred Congregation for the Propagation of the Faith issued norms regarding the foundation of indigenous religious congregations. Those norms provided a template for the constitutions of the congregations. The only points that were left for the founding generation to insert were the name and patrons of the congregation, its specific work, and the design of its habit.[48] Thus the ideals of radical gospel living and creative incarnation of the beatitudes were eroded by the desire for uniformity and for a ready supply of dedicated teachers, nurses, and other pastoral laborers. New communities of religious women were multiplied with a passion for service, along the same lines that had been successful in the past.

---

[47] McGlone, *Communidad Para El Mundo*, 29.

[48] S. Congregation Propaganda Fide, "Norme Della S. Congregazione De Propaganda Fide Per Redigere Le Costitutioni Di Nuove Congregazioni Di Diritto Diocesano Da Essa Dipendenti," in *Enchiridion Della Vita Consecrata: Dalle Decretali Al Rinnovamento Post-Conciliare (385–2000)*, Edizione Bilingue (Bologna: Ancora, 2001), 1080–1118.

The life came to be minutely regulated, dress and food were uniform, and a schedule, called an horarium, specified down to the quarter hour where each sister was expected to be and what she was expected to be doing from the time she awoke in the early morning, through a time of vocal prayer and mass, followed by breakfast, and a very active ministry. When the day was finished in the school or hospital, the sisters returned to the convent, where they continued their routine up to night prayers followed by Grand Silence, during which no one was permitted to speak except in an emergency. Certain periods of recreation were allowed in which the sisters were permitted to relax a bit, but they were often expected to catch up on household tasks or lesson planning during their recreation. Day after day, year after year, the life continued. To their credit, women dedicated themselves with incredible zeal and found a way to nourish lives of prayer and even deep spirituality within this regimen. Nevertheless, the life was increasingly out of touch with its cultural context, and many were calling for greater education and formation for the sisters.

Pius XII wrote and spoke often of the need for improvement in the lives of religious. In 1950 he wrote:

We find some other things in the institutes of women religious that are neither necessary nor complementary. Merely extrinsic and historical, they have their origin in the circumstances of former ages, and these conditions have greatly changed. When these things are no longer beneficial, or when they hinder a greater good, there does not appear to be any special reason for retaining them.[49]

Foremost in this movement for renewal in the United States was the work of the Sister Formation Conference, organized in 1954 under the leadership of Sister Ritamary Bradley, CHM, who described the mission of the conference as "Sister formation in all its aspects—spiritual, intellectual, and professional

---

[49] Pius XII, *Apostolic Constitution Sponsa Christi*, AAS 43 (1951) (Rome: Typis Polyglottis Vaticanis, 1950), no. 24.

training and their fitting integration in pre-service and in-service programs."[50]

These currents began the development of women religious in the United States from a corps of ready volunteer laborers in Catholic schools and hospitals into a well-educated cohort of professional women ready to engage the needs of society and of the church. In the course of this transformation Pope John XXIII announced on January 25, 1959, just three months after he became pope, that he would call an ecumenical council for the renewal of the church.[51]

THE SECOND VATICAN COUNCIL

The Second Vatican Council (1962–65) picked up Pope John's call for renewal expressed in his opening address to the first session of the council:

> The substance of the ancient doctrine of the deposit of faith is one thing, and the way in which it is presented is another. And it is the latter that must be taken into great consideration with patience if necessary, everything being measured in the forms and proportions of a Magisterium which is predominantly pastoral in character.[52]

The council's *Decree on the Adaptation and Renewal of Religious Life (Perfectae Caritatis)* gave further impetus and ecclesiastical legitimacy to a movement of renewal that had already begun, while the *Dogmatic Constitution on the Church (Lumen*

---

[50] Judith Ann Eby, *"A Little Squabble Among Nuns?": The Sister Formation Crisis and the Patterns of Authority and Obedience Among American Women Religious, 1954–1971* (St. Louis, MO: St. Louis University, 2000), 57.

[51] John XXIII, "Allocution Announcing the Roman Synod, The Ecumenical Council, and the Renewal of the Code of Canon Law, January 25, 1959," *AAS* 51 (1959): 65–69.

[52] John XXIII, "Allocution for the Opening of The Ecumenical Council," *AAS* 54 (1962), 792.

Gentium) situated religious life in the heart of its ecclesiology. This double task of internal renewal and renewed ecclesiology was taken up by religious with dedication and vigor.

Following the council, religious institutes began the task of renewal in earnest. The early twentieth century had been a time of homogenization of religious institutes, with women's communities mandated to conform their lives to myriad external and structural requirements.[53] The late twentieth century was a time to return to the sources of their founders, exploring the documents and stories of the founding generation. As the *Decree on the Adaptation and Renewal of Religious Life* puts it:

> The adaptation and renewal of the religious life includes both the constant return to the sources of all Christian life and to the original spirit of the institutes and their adaptation to the changed conditions of our time. (*PC*, no. 1)

The council called in the same document for a balancing of the gospel, the founding stories, developments in theology, the signs of the times, and the spirit of renewal (no. 2). In the process of renewal the council foresaw the need to involve all members of each institute, so that the renewal would not simply remain on paper, but would be an authentic renewal of the life and ministry of religious. Finally, the renewal process would include revision of the documents that regulated the life: "the constitutions, directories, custom books, books of prayers and ceremonies and such like" (no. 3).

Religious women undertook this work with diligence and dedication. Since the early 1950s, under the guidance of the Sister Formation Conference, sisters had been becoming better educated and more professionally prepared for ministry.[54] This

---

[53] Pii X pontificis maximi iussu digestus Benedicti papae XV auctoritate promulgatus, *Codex Iuris Canonici* (Rome: Tipografia poliglotta Vaticana, 1917); S. Congregation Propaganda Fide, "Norme Della S. Congregazione De Propaganda Fide Per Redigere Le Costitutioni Di Nuove Congregazioni Di Diritto Diocesano Da Essa Dipendenti."

[54] Eby, *A Little Squabble Among Nuns?*, 57.

preparation also suited them well to undertaking the task of a return to the sources of their institutes and to making a careful study of the founding generation and of the development of their charism and lifestyle over time. This prepared them for the task of discerning the key values of their founders and foundresses. They then turned to the task of reincarnating those values in their contemporary culture, with necessary adaptation, leaving aside those things that were "extrinsic and historical."[55] This also required a renewal of documents, and institutes undertook this work at general chapters and special chapters in the decades following the council.[56]

Renewed Ecclesiology

In examining the renewal of religious life following the Second Vatican Council, it is important to begin by examining the renewed ecclesiology of the council, found especially in the *Dogmatic Constitution on the Church*. This document was one of the principal achievements of the council, articulating the renewed understanding of the church called for by Pope John XXIII in the years leading up to the council.[57] Of the many images that have been used to describe the church, this document focuses on two of them: the church as mystery of salvation, and the church as people of God. Yves Congar expressed the shift this way: "Something happened at the Council and the dominant

---

[55] Pius XII, *Sponsa Christi*, no. 24.

[56] A chapter is a congregation-wide meeting of all members or a representation of the membership. "In an institute the general chapter has supreme authority in accordance with the constitutions. It is to be composed in such a way that it represents the whole institute and becomes a true sign of its unity in charity. Its principal functions are to protect the patrimony of the institute mentioned in Canon 578 and to foster appropriate renewal in accord with that patrimony. It also elects the supreme Moderator, deals with matters of greater importance, and issues norms which all are bound to obey" (Canon 631§1).

[57] John XXIII, "Allocution Announcing the Roman Synod, The Ecumenical Council, and the Renewal of the Code of Canon Law"; idem, *Humanae Salutis*; idem, "Allocution for the Opening of The Ecumenical Council."

values in our way of looking at the church were changed by the council."[58]

> At all times and in every race God has given welcome to whosoever honors God and does what is right. God, however, does not make people holy and save them merely as individuals, without bond or link between one another. Rather it has pleased God to bring them together as one people, a people which acknowledges God in truth and serves God in holiness. (*LG*, no. 9)

In discussing the people of God, the council takes up a scripture text that exhorts the early Christians to live up to their calling: "You are a chosen race, a royal priesthood, a holy nation, God's own people, in order that you may proclaim the mighty acts of him who called you out of darkness into his marvelous light. Once you were not a people, but now you are God's people" (1 Pt 2:9–10). Speaking of the priesthood of all the faithful, rooted in baptism and constituting a true participation in the priesthood of Christ, *Lumen Gentium* states:

> The baptized, by regeneration and the anointing of the Holy Spirit, are consecrated as a spiritual house and a holy priesthood. . . . The common priesthood of the faithful and the ministerial or hierarchical priesthood are nonetheless interrelated: each of them in its own special way is a participation in the one priesthood of Christ. (nos. 9–10)

The document goes on to explicitly speak of the work of God in other Christian churches, as well as among other religions and even those with no religion (nos. 15–16). This represented a true shift away from an image of church that saw its visible structures on earth as the only source of salvation, where the

---

[58] Yves Congar, "Moving Towards a Pilgrim Church," in *Vatican II by Those Who Were There*, ed. Alberic Stacpoole (London: Goeffrey Chapman, 1986), 129.

phrase "the church" meant the pope and the bishops, and the people were often seen as peripheral. Lumen Gentium went on to describe the role of collegiality among bishops in chapter 3, a chapter that was hotly debated during the council, and whose final wording represents a compromise between competing ideologies and ecclesiologies.

Chapters 4 and 5 take up again the topics of the lay Christian faithful and their call to holiness of life and to the work of continuing the mission of Jesus in their everyday lives. "This announcing of Christ by a living testimony as well as by the spoken word, takes on a specific quality and a special force in that it is carried out in the ordinary surroundings of the world" (no. 35).

The focus on lay Christians in this document came out of a growth in lay Christian movements that had always been a part of the church, but that had enjoyed a revitalization in the decades leading up to the Second Vatican Council. In turn, the resounding affirmation of the place of the laity in the church gave further encouragement to these movements and a reenergized sense of the mission and vocation of lay Christians. The ministry of the hierarchical church has sometimes been referred to as a participation in the ministry of Jesus as priest, prophet, and king. Lumen Gentium adds the insight that the whole people of God participates in the mission of Jesus as priest, prophet, and king. This notion is laid out particularly well in the *Catechism of the Catholic Church*, in its section on lay Christians.[59]

After speaking beautifully of the high calling of all Christians to holiness of life, to spirituality, and to bringing gospel values into their everyday lives, Lumen Gentium turns to a chapter on religious life. Continuing its self-reflection, it states, "the state of life which is constituted by the profession of the evangelical counsels, while not entering into the hierarchical structure of the Church, belongs undeniably to her life and holiness"

---

[59] John Paul II, *Catechism of the Catholic Church*, rev. ed (London: Geoffrey Chapman, 1999), 897–913.

(no. 43). In seeking to name what religious life is, the council pointed to the vows, also called the evangelical counsels. This appropriately focuses the discussion of consecrated life on the Gospels. In the Gospels, Jesus lived and taught a way of life rooted in prayer, community, and mission. The values that underlie the vows are found in the pages of the Gospels. All Christians are invited to the fullness of life proposed in the Gospels, but certain Christians take on a lifestyle that is framed by the obligations of practicing chastity in celibacy for the sake of the kingdom, poverty, and obedience. Vowed commitment to this lifestyle constitutes religious life as a particular way of living the Gospel and following Christ (nos. 42–43; *PC*, no. 1). The vows are not the life, but they are the context that enables a particular type of gospel living in community.

In baptism, Christians are born again of water and the spirit. It is hard to imagine a more radical incorporation into the life of Christ. Despite this, most church documents on consecrated life struggle to describe consecrated life as a life that is "more intimate," a "closer following," a "total dedication" (*PC*, no. 5). In the consecrated life, Christ's faithful, moved by the Holy Spirit, propose to follow Christ more nearly; to give themselves to God, who is loved above all; and, pursuing the perfection of charity in the service of the kingdom, to signify and proclaim in the church the glory of the world to come.[60] Religious life is what the church is, *only more of it.*

The council closed on December 8, 1965. We have traced two important notions in the council documents, namely, its statements on religious life, and its self-reflection on the nature of the church, particularly on the laity within the church. Next we turn to a discussion of the reception of these elements of the council teaching in the church in the United States in the decades following the council.

---

[60] John Paul II, *Code of Canon Law: Latin-English Edition, New English Translation* (Washington DC: Canon Law Society of America, 1983), canon 573.

Reception of Vatican II

In *In Spiritu Sancto,* the apostolic brief officially closing the Second Vatican Council, Paul VI solemnly declared:

> [The council] must be numbered without doubt among the greatest events of the Church. The largest in the number of fathers that came to the See of Peter from every part of the world, even from those places where the hierarchy has been very recently established. It was the richest because of the questions which have been discussed carefully and profoundly for four sessions. And last of all it was the most opportune, because, bearing in mind the necessities of the present day, above all it sought to meet pastoral needs. Nourishing the flame of charity, it has made a great effort to reach not only the Christians still separated from communion with the Holy See, but also the whole human family.

After the close of the council the work of implementation began in earnest, opening a period of profound changes in the lives of Catholics around the globe. In the tumultuous 1960s, the liturgical renewal was implemented, texts were translated, and people were invited into a broader participation in the liturgical life of the church. Prior to the council, the mass had been the timeless, changeless icon at the heart of the life of each parish. Almost overnight, the entire look and feel of the mass changed dramatically for the first time in living memory. Liturgists and scholars were quick to point out that the familiar rituals that were being left behind were themselves the product of a historical development, and reflected the culture and theological innovations of a previous century. Clergy and people alike strove to understand and keep pace with the changes.

The *Decree on the Adaptation and Renewal of Religious Life* had been a minor document of the council; it had not been closely debated on the council floor. Like all the documents of the council, a working document had been prepared before the council, and in this case it was ratified with little discussion or modification. Nevertheless, this document was received by religious institutes of women in the United States that were ripe for renewal.

The Sister Formation Movement[61] had successfully promoted the increased education and formation of women religious in the 1950s and 1960s so that sisters became the most educated group of women the world had ever seen. They were theologically prepared to engage the call for renewal and embraced the task of returning to the sources of religious life, renewing it and stripping away years of customs and practices that had long outlived their usefulness. Earlier, in 1950, in *Sponsa Christi,* Pius XII had invited women religious to let go of elements that were "merely extrinsic and historical, they have their origin in the circumstances of former ages, and these conditions have greatly changed" (no. 24). By the close of the council, sisters were ready to embrace this call to action.

Religious women were more numerous than they had been at any point in the history of religious life in the United States, with nearly 180,000[62] sisters in 1965, when the council closed. At that time there were about 960,000 religious women globally.[63] The largest groups ever to enter their communities were entering in the years before, during, and shortly after the Second Vatican Council. With the newly launched focus on education and professional development, these women enthusiastically received the call of the council and began the task of study, reflection, and discussion with a view to renewing and adapting their lives and their constitutions. The records of chapter meetings over these years demonstrate the seriousness with which they undertook the task.

---

[61] Eby, *A Little Squabble Among Nuns?*

[62] "Frequently Requested Church Statistics," Center for Applied Research in the Apostolate—Georgetown University, 2012, georgetown.edu website.

[63] Angel Pardilla, "Le Religiose Dopo Il Concilio: Dati Statistici (1965–2005)," *Commentarium Pro Religiosis Et Missionariis* 90, nos. 1–2 (2009): 29–90.

Prior to Vatican II, chapters tended to examine details of clothing, schedule, and other matters of internal organization of their highly structured life. After the council, chapters sought to explore the core identity of religious women in the twentieth century and to renew and reinvigorate that life. The task of renewal culminated in the rewriting of constitutions that could not be finalized until the promulgation of the revised *Code of Canon Law* in 1983. It is interesting to trace the focus of chapters after the decades of renewal. In those chapters the focus of reflection and deliberation shifts outward to mission and to justice and earth concerns. Much less time is spent on matters of the identity and life of the sisters.[64]

This task of renewal was undertaken when the median age of most women religious in the United States was in the forties.[65] Women were young, energetic, and idealistic. While these years were filled with expansive hopes, they were also marked with significant challenges. Many women religious left their communities during these turbulent years. Some left in anger or frustration with the renewal process; it was going too fast, too slow, or going in altogether the wrong direction for them. Some took the universal call to holiness and mission as a reason for letting go of the structures of religious life while remaining committed to ministry and to lives of spirituality and holiness. Some sought independence from the structures of religious life, realizing they weren't called, or wanting to pursue a career that would have been unthinkable just a few decades before.

During this period thousands of religious in hundreds of communities explored, read, debated, and wrote about the meaning of religious life, their foundation and charism, its expression, adaptation, and renewal. To trace but one publication, *Review for Religious* began publication in 1942. During the years

---

[64] "Chapter Documents 1950–2010" (St. Louis, MO, n.d.), Sisters of St. Joseph of Carondelet-St. Louis Province Archives.

[65] Sandra M. Schneiders, "That Was Then . . . This Is Now," lecture delivered at the Women and Spirit Exhibit, University of Notre Dame, Indiana, September 24, 2011.

following the council, it doubled the number of articles published each year, with articles treating every phase of religious life. Peaking in the 1980s, the journal began a slow decline, with fewer articles by and for religious and more articles on general spirituality. It finally ceased publication altogether in 2012.

Beyond Renewal

The flurry of activity following the council with the renewal of religious life and its documents began in the 1960s and continued through the 1970s, peaking with the completion of work on the constitutions and their final approval in the 1980s. During this time there had been significant numbers of women leaving religious life, and new applicants slowed to a trickle. Communities that once boasted fifty or more new members a year were lucky to get one or two during this period. By 1975, there were 25 percent fewer women religious than there were at the high point just ten years before, in 1965. This was due to departures and fewer new members coupled with attrition through death. The decline in numbers slowed, and the number of women religious declined only 15 percent in the next decade. In recent decades numbers have decreased as the large Vatican II cohort ages. The years from 2000 to 2010 experienced the loss of 34 percent of women religious in the United States.[66] In addition to acknowledging the numerical decline, it is important to take time to grieve the loss of so many brilliant and dedicated women who built the Catholic school system and Catholic healthcare, and deeply touched the hearts and lives of countless people in the church and in society. They witnessed to strong, prophetic leadership and paved the way for women in the ministry of the church and in many professions. They also opened the doors to lay teachers, healthcare providers, and pastoral ministers in today's church. They continue to be held in high esteem by many for their courageous and persevering witness to gospel values.

---

[66] "Frequently Requested Church Statistics."

Housing arrangements also changed during this time, as sisters moved out of large institutional convents into smaller local communities. The larger communities had as many as fifty or more sisters living in the same house, perhaps working in a school or hospital nearby, or fanning out to various ministries in the region. Life had been highly regulated, and in addition to a full-time ministry, sisters were expected to fulfill a regimen of prayers in common, community meals, and other convent duties. The small communities usually had five to ten sisters who were able to adapt their lives and schedules to meet the changing needs of the group and adjust to the new understandings of their lives. Some found these changes infused new life into their communities. Over time, many communities got smaller as the total number of sisters declined, and there were fewer large facilities capable of housing more than three to five sisters. Parish convents were converted to other uses, and sisters had to find other living arrangements in houses or apartments where zoning regulations frequently prohibited more than a few sisters living in the same unit.

Ministry also changed as a consequence of the renewal. Religious women had built the Catholic hospital system and been the major players in the establishment of a flourishing Catholic school system. During the early days of religious life in the United States, sisters had gone to the fringes of society and sought to serve unmet needs of the pioneer, Native American, and immigrant communities. The Catholic school system educated generations of Catholics, playing a major part in moving immigrant Catholics into the mainstream of American life and into every profession. This had its symbolic high point when John F. Kennedy became the first Catholic to serve as president of the United States. During the years after the council, sisters turned more and more to other ministries and to populations that were at greater risk. This move, together with the decreasing numbers of sisters, left positions unfilled in their institutions. Some of these closed, but the majority remained open as lay men and women came to serve as educators and healthcare professionals. Thus the universal call to mission articulated by the council found practical expression as lay people dedicated themselves in increasing numbers to the mission of education and healthcare.

Over time, the sisters moved off the floor of the hospitals and out of the classrooms into administrative positions in their institutions. As numbers continued to decline, they entrusted the administration increasingly to lay people and retained a few seats on largely lay boards of directors and trustees. Even finding sisters able to serve on boards is becoming a challenge, and religious communities are seeking ways to transition to completely lay-run institutions.

In one Midwest high school academy, a common story is being played out. Built in the 1950s, the academy was staffed almost completely by sisters who lived in the convent on the same property. Over time, more and more lay staff took their places alongside the sisters, who continued in fewer numbers, mentoring their collaborators in dedication to education as a ministry and in a gospel-based call to service. Until recently a few elderly sisters lived in the convent, while the school was staffed by dedicated professional lay teachers. Now the remaining sisters are moving to a retirement facility and yielding the property to the academy to further its mission. Similar stories are being played out in the countless schools and hospitals built by sisters across the country. While there are elements of decline in this period, there is also a meta-story of inviting and mentoring men and women in taking their place in the mission of the church. Through these efforts we now have educated and empowered professional lay ecclesial ministers. This has called for changes and professionalization of the ministries as the mission continues.

All of these changes in the lives of sisters gradually gave rise to a new ecclesial reality. Many of the religious institutes that were serving in hospitals and schools were founded in an era when there were vast unmet social needs. Now there is a huge and still growing number of men and women serving in ministries previously staffed almost entirely by sisters. Empowered lay professionals have taken their places in the mission of the church in unprecedented numbers. There is a growing nonprofit sector that is providing an immense range of services in communities across the country. In addition, social entrepreneurs are finding ways of embedding social benefit into business enterprises, ensuring the sustainability of the social benefit they provide. If the goal of mission activity is "to work yourself out of a job," then the sisters have been amazingly successful. And yet it may well be asked: what is the ongoing relevance of ministerial religious life in a church that has come to recognize more fully the universal call to holiness and to mission?

Some of those observing religious life today engage in a discourse of failure, questioning the decrease in the numbers of sisters from a high of 180,000 in 1965 to less than one-third of that number in 2012. Over this same time period the US population has risen by 60 percent, and the US Catholic population has risen by 50 percent.[67] Some claim that the decline in numbers of women religious is the result of some failure on the part of these women and their communities, while others point to a number of social and ecclesial factors that have contributed to this change.[68] These factors include increasing opportunities for ministry and service and, for women, increasing professional opportunities in general. Many options for ministry that are open to women today were unthinkable just fifty years ago. Another factor is the decreasing religious affiliation among Gen X and Millennials, the two generations with significantly lower numbers entering religious life. These generations are less religiously affiliated than their parents and grandparents were when they were young.[69] Young people also have fewer and fewer opportunities to interact with religious, especially religious who are within their own generation. In the 1960s, there was one woman religious for every 250 Catholics. In 2012,

---

[67] US Population Census (Washington DC: US Census Bureau, 2012); and "Frequently Requested Church Statistics."

[68] Schneiders, "That Was Then . . . This Is Now."

[69] *Religion Among the Millennials* (Washington DC: Pew Research Center, February 2010).

there is one woman religious for every 1,200 Catholics. If we look at age cohorts, in 2012, 60 percent of Catholics were under the age of fifty-five, whereas only 7 percent of religious women were under the age of fifty-five.[70] Sisters may one day be one in a million. Young people today are much less likely to know sisters or to interact with them than young people in the 1960s.

CONCLUSION

All these changes point to the imperative that religious life meet its changed circumstances. Surveying two thousand years of religious life affords a panoramic view of a life that is stable yet always reinventing itself. Each of these reinventions arose because of changed circumstances and the need for a new response from religious. The radical shifts in religious life and in the culture of today are calling for yet another reinvention, a new form of the life that will not supplant the former, as each of the prior forms have continued to exist alongside the old. The reinventions have changed the structures, leadership, and the level of centralization. They have changed the vows that formed the context for the life and the size and stability of the community. They have changed the structure of the day; the ministerial focus; and the balance of prayer, community, and ministry. Nonetheless, at the heart, throughout all the changes, religious life remains a life radically committed to incarnating the gospel here and now, living the beatitudes, and bringing the love of God to ever new frontiers.

---

[70] "Frequently Requested Church Statistics"; *Statistical Report* (Washington DC: National Religious Retirement Office, August 2012).

CHAPTER TWO

THEOLOGY OF COMMUNITY

One of the key elements of emerging religious life is community. Yet the issue of community transcends religious life. Social commentators have identified the loss and quest for community as key issues in understanding society today. In the late 1980s, a Notre Dame Study on Parish Life discussed this issue:

> Social commentators identify loss of a sense of community as a central problem of our times. Society has gotten complex and crowded. Work is often specialized, anonymous, and its products distant. Residential life is privatized, often far removed from work life or civic involvements.[1]

Yet even in our privatized, individualized society, many people yearn for a life-giving experience of community. It would be naive to expect that a handful of well-meaning people can come together and expect community to develop naturally or by the operation of some set of rules that they agree upon.[2] Community takes commitment and sustained effort on the part of the members. This project can take inspiration from some twentieth-century visionaries such as Dietrich Bonhoeffer, Brother Roger of Taizé, Dorothy Day, and Jean Vanier, who all saw that community is a key to living the Christian life in today's world.

---

[1] David C. Leege, "The Parish as Community," *The Notre Dame Study of Catholic Parish Life* 10 (March 1987): 1.

[2] See Jean Vanier, *Community and Growth*, 2nd rev. ed. (Mahwah, NJ: Paulist Press, 1989), 11. Cited hereafter as *C&G*.

This chapter briefly examines the life of each of these individuals and some of their writings. It attempts to draw out some common threads of their thought, beginning to articulate a theology of community. The first two writers we examine come from the Reform tradition, so it is important to note that Martin Luther (1483–1546) had rejected monasticism, though he himself entered an Augustinian monastery at the age of twenty-two. He was excommunicated twenty-two years later and would later repudiate monasticism as a life form. Luther and other reformers rejected the notion that a person could earn salvation through the monastic practices and the life of asceticism.[3] This anti-monastic bent is part of the heritage of the Reformation and helps explain the nearly complete absence of monasticism in most reformed churches. This would also be an important part of the heritage of Dietrich Bonhoeffer and Roger Schutz, as they began to think about the importance of Christian community in the first half of the twentieth century. The next two writers, Dorothy Day and Jean Vanier, came out of the Catholic tradition. They began their work in community at a time when religious life was flourishing in North America, and large groups of new members were swelling the ranks of most religious communities. Nevertheless, they sought to form a different kind of community. For each of the writers, it is important to see what they drew from the tradition of Christian community found in religious life and what they left aside as they sought to build their movements.

DIETRICH BONHOEFFER
AND THE NEW MONASTICISM

Dietrich Bonhoeffer (1906–45) was a German Lutheran pastor and theologian noted for his resistance to the Nazi regime at a

---

[3] Thomas P. Rausch, *Radical Christian Communities* (Collegeville, MN: Liturgical Press, 1990), 84–88; Martin Luther, "De Votis Monasticis" (Wittenberg, 1521); John Calvin, *Institutes of the Christian Religion*, trans. Henry Beveridge (London: Arnold Hatfield, 1599), 4:13.

time when many church leaders were taking a more conciliatory stance, seeking to preserve church independence in the increasingly oppressive Germany. The Nazis imprisoned him and then executed him shortly before the end of the war.

Bonhoeffer began his pastoral work in Germany during the rise of Nazism. In community he and others found the wisdom and courage to confront the horrific situation around them. They sought to live the gospel with fidelity and to challenge both church and state to stop the violence and the genocidal program of the Nazi regime. This commitment proved to be demanding, costing Bonhoeffer and some of his collaborators their lives. Bonhoeffer believed in the importance of banding together for mutual support in living the gospel. In a letter to his brother Karl-Friedrich, Bonhoeffer wrote:

> The restoration of the church will surely come only from a new type of monasticism which has nothing in common with the old but a complete lack of compromise in a life lived in accordance with the Sermon on the Mount in the discipleship of Christ. I think it is time to gather people together to do this.[4]

Bonhoeffer had his opportunity to begin an experiment in new monasticism when he taught at Finkenwalde from 1935 to 1937. A seminary had been organized there to preserve Christian theology and practice that had been abandoned by the Nazi-inspired German Evangelical Church. Seminarians spent six months at the underground seminary where, in addition to serious reading and study of gospel values, they practiced life in community. While they studied theology and the scriptures, they actively and deliberately sought to live the gospel and to engage one another in this commitment. Finkenwalde "brought together the basic components of the seminarians' experience— personal and corporate meditation, prayer, solitude, Bible study,

---

[4] Dietrich Bonhoeffer, letter to Karl-Friedrich Bonhoeffer, in *A Testament to Freedom*, 424, quoted in Eberhard Bethge, *Bonhoeffer: Exile and Martyr*, ed. J. W. de Gruchy (London: Collins, 1975), 53.

fellowship, singing, recreation, ministry, worship, the eucharist, confession and spiritual care."[5]

After the Nazis forced Finkenwalde to close in 1937, Bonhoeffer wrote one of his more popular works, *Life Together*. In this book Bonhoeffer reflects on the principles that had guided the community at Finkenwalde and that he had sought to live there. Surrounded by the hostile Nazi regime, the community sought a life true to the gospel, and to provide support for one another in this project. Bonhoeffer shows remarkable insight into the blessings and challenges of living community. Community is the privileged place of meeting Christ, and supporting one another in the journey to God. In some respects, *Life Together* resembles a monastic rule, written to outline the practices of the community, to give insight into the fundamentals of Christian life in community, and to inspire its members to take advantage of the gift of community.

Life Together is divided into five chapters treating community, the day together, the day alone, service, and confession and the Lord's Supper. In speaking of community Bonhoeffer says, "The Christian cannot simply take for granted the privilege of living among other Christians."[6] Many people do not have the gift of likeminded, committed Christians with whom to share life. Many people have the opportunity to have good community at some time in their life, and we all should welcome and celebrate this gift when we have the opportunity to live community "through Jesus Christ and in Jesus Christ."[7] Far from the emotional high of a weekend retreat or service project, the commitment to live community on an ongoing basis requires deliberate and persevering effort. It is rewarding, but Bonhoeffer is quick to point out the challenges of living community not

---

[5] Susan Rakoczy, "The Witness of Community Life: Bonhoeffer's *Life Together* and the Taizé Community," *Journal of Theology for Southern Africa* 127 (2007): 48.

[6] Dietrich Bonhoeffer, *Life Together* (New York: Harper and Row, 1954), 27. Cited hereafter as *LT*.

[7] *LT*, 31.

simply for our own purposes and personal needs. When we choose to live in community, we set out on a journey together in Christ. In his famous work *The Cost of Discipleship*, Bonhoeffer pointed out the role of monastic community in the history of Christianity. Monasteries, as the Christian communities of their day, were a living witness to the challenges of taking the Gospel and its demands seriously:

> The expansion of Christianity and the increasing secularization of the church caused the awareness of costly grace to be gradually lost. . . . But the Roman church did keep a remnant of that original awareness. It was decisive that monasticism did not separate from the church and that the church had the good sense to tolerate monasticism. Here, on the boundary of the church, was the place where the awareness that grace is costly and that grace includes discipleship was preserved. . . . Monastic life thus became a living protest against the secularization of Christianity, against the cheapening of grace.[8]

The community is a local expression of the church as the community of faith. Community members call us out of ourselves, toward the other, to strengthen one another. "The Christ in their own hearts is weaker than the Christ in the word of other Christians."[9] Together, Christians form the body of Christ in community, mediating Christ to one another.

Bonhoeffer devotes a substantial portion of the chapter on the day together to common prayer (80 percent in the original German). He discusses the order of service, the importance of praying the psalms, *lectio continua* or the sequential reading of scripture, and his opinions on congregational singing. This section of the book seems to have echoes of the rule of Benedict,

---

[8] Dietrich Bonhoeffer, *The Cost of Discipleship* (Bel Air, CA: Touchstone, 1995), 46.

[9] *LT*, 332.

chapters 8–19, where Benedict makes detailed arrangements for the praying of the psalms in the Divine Office.

The remaining pages of the chapter on the day together are devoted to the common meal and to work that may be alone or in groups.

> The breaking of bread together has a festive quality. . . . It is our daily bread that we eat, not my own. We share our bread. Thus we are firmly bound to one another not only in the Spirit, but with our whole physical being. . . . As long as we eat our bread together, we will have enough even with the smallest amount. Hunger begins only when people desire to keep their own bread for themselves.[10]

The common table is an important part of Christian life in community. It is simple nourishment for us. It is nourishment for the life of the community. It is a sharing of goods with the poor. It is a metaphor for the global sharing of goods in which all share what they have and all receive what they need. It is also a metaphor for the eucharistic table at which we receive the fullness of life here and in eternity.

Nourished in Spirit by common prayer and nourished in body and spirit by the common meal, the Christian community goes to work. By the work of their hands and hearts and minds, Christians engage the world around them, earn their daily bread, and do the work of the gospel as they seek to build a more just and sustainable world. There is a natural rhythm of the day that moves from prayer to work and back to prayer again.

> Prayer should not be hindered by work, but neither should work be hindered by prayer. Just as it was God's will that human beings should work six days and rest and celebrate before the face of God on the seventh, so it is also God's

---

[10] *LT*, 73–74 (citing Mt 6:11, "Give us this day our daily bread").

will that every day should be marked for the Christian both by prayer and work.[11]

Though the Finkenwalde community consisted of students and faculty of the seminary, Bonhoeffer seems to have manual labor in mind when he talks about work. "Work puts human beings in the world of things,"[12] he says. In discussing work, Bonhoeffer alludes to the writings of Martin Buber, who distinguishes between I-It relationships and I-Thou relationships.[13] When we relate as I-Thou we relate as person to person, we relate with another person as other, not as a function of ourselves but as a distinct human being or as God. This is the way we relate in prayer and in community. But in work Bonhoeffer sees us as relating to "the world of things." In this way work can bring us out of self and keep us honest, "this new encounter frees [us] for objectivity."[14]

> The work of the world can only be accomplished where people forget themselves, where they lose themselves in a cause, reality, the task, the It. Christians learn at work to allow the task to set the bounds for them.[15]

This is clearly the case with manual labor, but the work of many people brings them into relationship with other people. Even in working with things, we often interact with others with whom and for whom we work. Yet there is certainly a distinct character of work that sets it apart from the life of prayer and shared meals and times of shared life in community. It is the goal or the reality of the task with which we relate. Work is done or not done; it is well done, or it has mistakes. It has an

---

[11] *LT*, 74–75.

[12] *LT*, 75.

[13] Martin Buber, *I and Thou*, trans. Walter Kaufmann (Bel Air, CA: Touchstone, 1971), 54, 62, 66.

[14] *LT*, 75.

[15] *LT*, 80.

objectivity that offers a counterpoint to the subjectivity and intersubjectivity of prayer and relationships in community.

Bonhoeffer then turns to a chapter on the day alone. Solitude is essential for community, yet solitude also presents some challenges. Bonhoeffer has harsh words for those who use community only for their own needs, as a form of escape:

> Many persons seek community because they are afraid of loneliness. . . . Because they can no longer endure being alone, such people are driven to seek the company of other people. . . . More often than not, they are disappointed. . . . Whoever cannot be alone should beware of community. Whoever cannot stand being in community should beware of being alone.[16]

Bonhoeffer draws a parallel between solitude and community, on the one hand, and silence and speech, on the other. "Genuine speech comes out of silence and genuine silence comes out of speech."[17] In the "silence before the word" the individual can engage in personal meditation on the word and be confronted by the power of the Word of God. In addition, silence is essential for those who live "close together in a confined space." They need the space for personal renewal so that they are able to be better community members. During this time alone, all community members were exhorted to be alone and not to disturb one another.[18]

Time alone has three purposes: "meditation on the scripture, prayer, and intercession."[19] Bonhoeffer urges communal reading of full chapters of scripture to be complemented by personal reflection on shorter passages, or even a single word or phrase. He also gives great importance to intercessory prayer, for oneself, for others in community, for those served through ministry, and

---

[16] *LT*, 76–77.
[17] *LT*, 83.
[18] *LT*, 123.
[19] *LT*, 86.

for the wider world community. He sees intercession as a duty that we owe to one another. He expresses disdain for those who give over their time alone to self-indulgent rumination and even questions the inclination to deeper forms of prayer that leave aside meditation on the word and intercession.[20]

Bonhoeffer next turns to the life of service. In community one can learn the simple ways of gracious living together, which is a life of service within and beyond the community. Coming into community, it is not long before one begins to see the weaknesses of others. This is a challenge to growth in service. We learn first to remain silent in the face of others' misdeeds, while growing in meekness and learning the virtue of helpfulness. This is also an occasion to confront personal weakness and grow in our own Christian commitment. As we come to a place of maturity, wisdom, and gentleness, we are able to speak a good word to our brothers and sisters to help them along on their journey. And only then are we ready to go out into the wider community to preach the gospel in a meaningful way.[21]

The final chapter is a somewhat lengthy discussion of the importance of confession, by which Bonhoeffer means the confession of personal weakness and sin to another person in community. This is somewhat like the Catholic sacramental confession, but Bonhoeffer does not believe that only one person in a community should be charged with receiving the confession of all the others. He believes this approach sets up an unhealthy power dynamic that is too ripe for abuse. At the same time, he recognizes that while, in theory, every Christian should be able to receive the confession of another, in practice it requires a spiritual maturity and that some will be more gifted in this ministry than others. Bonhoeffer also distinguishes the practice of confessing only to God. Confessing to another person is made with the purpose of confessing to God and being forgiven by God. It helps to break through self-deception:

---

[20] *LT*, 92.
[21] *LT*, 94, 97.

> We must ask ourselves whether we often have not been
> deluding ourselves about our confession of sin to God—
> whether we have not instead been confessing our sins to
> ourselves and also forgiving ourselves. . . . As long as I
> am by myself when I confess my sins, everything remains
> in the dark; but when I come face to face with another
> Christian, the sin has to be brought to the light.[22]

Bonhoeffer's notion of confession bears a similarity to step five of the Twelve Step program of Alcoholics Anonymous: "Admitted to God, to ourselves, and to another human being the exact nature of our wrongs."[23] Both recognize that confession to another human being is a profound experience of self-revelation, which helps a person to be free of the domination of personal sin and weakness. "Sin isolates us in order to have dominion."[24]

The Finkenwalde experience profoundly shaped Bonhoeffer's vision of the church as community. He expressed his ecclesiology very clearly in his short book *Life Together*. The book "brought together the basic components of the seminarians' experience—personal and corporate meditation, prayer, solitude, Bible study, fellowship, singing, recreation, ministry, worship, the eucharist, confession and spiritual care."[25] Bonhoeffer explores the constellation of values and practices that are necessary for building Christian community and also helps to demonstrate the powerful effect of community for those who live it. He also shares his conviction of the need of Christian community in his own day, a need that is even more profound in contemporary church and society.

In reflecting on community Bonhoeffer recognized the importance of integrating solitude and community in life and

---

[22] *LT*, 112–13.

[23] Alcoholics Anonymous, *Twelve Steps and Twelve Traditions* (New York: AA World Services, 2002), 55.

[24] *LT*, 112.

[25] Rakoczy, "The Witness of Community Life," 48.

in prayer. He had examined some forms of Catholic and Anglican monastic life before his experience at Finkenwalde and clearly valued the core elements of this lifestyle, as is evident from his desire to establish "a new type of monasticism."[26] Hence, it is interesting to note those elements of community he considered central to this project and those he left aside. *Life Together* emphasizes the importance of common prayer, common meals and shared property, and of the spiritual practice of confession. It also devotes some pages to personal growth in community and to communion among members. But in his treatment of community, Bonhoeffer does not mention the subject of authority and obedience or vowed celibacy, though these are common elements of other monastic communities. The community existed within the seminary structures, which probably precluded any need to mention the subject of authority further in *Life Together*. Also, because seminarians were in community for a set period of time, a commitment to celibacy did not seem to fit the transitory community they were building. Bonhoeffer notes that communities that exist for a shorter period of time are relatively easier to build than those that remain together for years or even for a lifetime.[27] Nevertheless, *Life Together* remains a brief but profound reflection on the nature of radical Christian community in the midst of a hostile society.

The term *new monasticism* has been taken up by the increasing number of radical Christian communities that are gathering today in Europe and North America. Members of this movement have begun to network among themselves, develop an understanding of common elements, and share insights into living community in the twenty-first century. Later in this book we explore their insights and ask what they have to say to those living religious life into the heart of the twenty-first century.

---

[26] Bonhoeffer, letter to Karl-Friedrich Bonhoeffer, in *A Testament to Freedom*, 424, quoted in Bethge, *Bonhoeffer*, 53.

[27] *LT*, 24.

BROTHER ROGER AND THE TAIZÉ COMMUNITY

Brother Roger Schutz (1915–2005) began his project in Christian community a few years after Bonhoeffer's community was disbanded and the seminary at Finkenwalde was closed. Schutz was born of a Swiss father and a French mother in Provence. His father was a Protestant pastor who taught his son an openness to other religious traditions. In his theology studies Brother Roger was interested in monasticism and studied the early monastic rules.[28] Also from his early days he conceived the idea of establishing a community. In 1940, in the midst of World War II, he purchased a house in the village of Taizé, in northern France. Two others joined him shortly thereafter. Two years later they fled to Switzerland and returned after the liberation of France. In 1944, they began a rhythm of prayer and community that would come to characterize the Taizé movement. It wasn't till 1949 that the first seven brothers, including Brother Roger, made public profession, promising to live in community as brothers, to hold their goods in common, to practice celibacy, and to be guided by Brother Roger's leadership. A few years later Brother Roger wrote the rule of Taizé, which briefly outlines the principles behind the life of the community. The rule is deliberately brief because Brother Roger believed that the community must never forfeit the responsibility of seeking and following God's will anew each day. He wrote:

> The purpose of a rule is to create a profound unity for him who perseveres, who is ready to give up perpetual discussion, and make a fresh beginning again and again, for the Christian life is but a constant re-beginning, a return to grace every day, sometimes even every hour, through

---

[28] Roger Schutz, *Brother Roger of Taizé: Essential Writings*, ed. Marcello Fidanzio, Modern Spiritual Masters Series (Maryknoll, NY: Orbis Books, 2006), 18.

Him who, after each failure, pardons us so that all things should be made new.[29]

The Taizé community continued to grow and, beginning in the 1960s, it became a place of pilgrimage for young adults who were losing their confidence in the Christian roots of Europe. The brothers listened to them and sought to rediscover for and with them reasons for hope. Angelo Roncalli, later Pope John XXIII, met with the brothers in 1958 and praised Taizé as "that little springtime." He later invited Brother Roger to be an observer at the Second Vatican Council.[30] There are now about seventy professed brothers at Taizé and a community of Catholic sisters nearby.

Brother Roger's vision for the community is to do everything "for the sake of Christ and the Gospel." The name of Christ appears fifty-two times in the rule, which has 4,369 words in its English translation. The centrality of Christ is a fundamental evangelical stance that informs the entire project of Taizé and its rule. The community gathers for mutual support on the path of gospel living, and the brothers in community are able to rely on one another's love, prayer, and help along the way. In the prologue of the rule Brother Roger says to the brothers: "From now on you are no longer alone. In all things, you must take your brothers into account."[31]

This chapter examines the rule of Taizé in an effort to understand this movement and its insights into Christian community. The rule is minimalistic: "This rule contains the minimum needed for a community to grow up in Christ and devote itself to a common service of God." Brother Roger acknowledges that allowing this broad freedom can open the door to having "a pretext for living according to your own impulses." Yet he

---

[29] Roger Schutz, *This Day Belongs to God* (London: Mowbray, 1972), 25.

[30] Rakoczy, "The Witness of Community Life," 56.

[31] Brother Roger, *Parable of Community: The Rule and Other Basic Texts of Taizé* (reprint, New York: Seabury Press, 1981), 9, 11. Cited hereafter as *RT*.

nevertheless kept this minimalist style because if he specified everything, he believed that it would exempt the community from its primary obligation, the daily effort to seek and follow the will of God. "Better run this risk [of minimalism], and not settle into complacency and routine."[32]

After the foreword the various elements of the community are grouped in sections in the short rule: (1) common practices, common prayer, common meals, and the council of the brothers; (2) exhortations regarding personal holiness, focusing on inner silence, and the spirit of the beatitudes; (3) practices that are analogous to the religious vows: sharing of goods, celibacy, and the role of the prior; (4) practicalities of brothers on mission, new brothers, and guests; and finally, (5) the exhortations and commitments of the profession ceremony of a new brother.

Community practices color the daily life of the brothers. Prayer has a central place in the life of the community. The typical liturgy of Taizé developed gradually over time and came to include a flowing together of the word, praying the psalms, brief repetitive chants, and extended periods of silence in community. The music of Taizé and its liturgical style have inspired many people across the globe. The music has a strong attraction and ministry to young adults. The brothers use a white robe for their common prayer: "The liturgical vestment is worn to remind us that our whole being has been clothed by Christ. It is a way of expressing our praise of the Lord other than by words." This is indicative of the style of Taizé, where prayer includes not only words and singing, but also candles, icons, incense, clothing, and the presence of the many pilgrims and guests of various lands and languages, all united in the worship space. Taizé's spirituality of the liturgy views the assembly gathered in prayer as consciously present in the midst of the communion of saints and in union with the whole Christian community. This also reflects the ecumenical approach of Taizé which is one of living communion, even if it is a communion which is marred by historical divisions. Brother Roger's ecumenical vocation is

---

[32] *RT*, 11, 11, 40.

shared by the whole community: "Never resign yourself to the scandal of the separation of Christians, who also readily confess love for their neighbor, and yet remain divided. Be consumed with burning zeal for the unity of the Body of Christ."[33] Community prayer flows seamlessly into personal prayer and into the other parts of the day, and back again into common prayer.

The council of brothers is made up of the professed brothers of the community and is the governing body of the community at Taizé. The rule sets the tone for the council, situating it in silence and listening. "The first step is to bring yourself into silence, to be ready to listen to your Lord." From this posture, the rule exhorts the brothers to avoid all semblance of politics, but instead to present their views simply and sincerely. Presiding over the council, the prior ensures the unity of the assembly, even as the various ideas and opinions are freely voiced. The section on the council comes before the section on the prior, who is seen primarily as the servant of communion and secondarily as the one who makes decisions on behalf of the community, but only after hearing the brothers assembled in council. In the council of brothers, all the brothers are expected to be present, to share their opinion with the prior, or to nominate a proxy.[34]

The brothers are exhorted to inner silence to cultivate their attitude of listening to the word of God and to enable this attitude to permeate and enrich the work and other activities of the day. The rule acknowledges the challenge of silence and cautions the brothers to accept the challenges of inner silence: "Who does not dread this silence?"[35] Yet the rule urges the brothers not to avoid silence through work or other activities or through filling it with useless diversions, but by staying in the silence, they will come to a deep spirit of prayer and of communion with God.

The spirit of the beatitudes is a powerful call for the brothers, particularly the values of joy, mercy, and simplicity. Joy and love

---

[33] *RT*, 15, 13.
[34] *RT*, 18, 18–19, 34.
[35] *RT*, 22.

are the two most frequent values mentioned in the rule. The rule speaks glowingly of joy, while it cautions against the harshness and cynicism that can emerge when people live closely in community year after year:

> True joy begins within.
>
> Acting the fool has never restored joy. Remember that there is no clear dividing line between simple joking and the irony which turns a smile into a grimace. Mockery, the poison of common life, is perfidious because it serves to cloak so-called truths which nobody would dare to express in direct conversation. It is cowardly, because it demolishes a brother in front of others.
>
> Perfect joy lies in the utter simplicity of peaceful love. In order to shine out, such joy requires no less than your whole being.[36]

Likewise, the section on mercy provides sage advice on good relations in community, on forgiveness, and on being forgiven. The rule also prescribes the practice of confession to "one of the brothers chosen with the prior,"[37] though there is no description of the practice.

Next the rule turns to three practices that are analogous to the three vows practiced in religious institutes, namely, celibacy, community of goods, and the role of the prior. Celibacy is practiced so that the brothers may have "greater freedom to attend to the things of God." Celibacy does not detract from the value of human relationships, which remain an important part of life together in community and in society. In addition, the rule gives some attention to cultivating purity of heart. Analogous to the vow of poverty is the community of goods: "The pooling of goods is total. The audacity involved in putting to good use all that is available at any time, not laying up

---

[36] *RT*, 25.
[37] *RT*, 28.

capital and not fearing possible poverty, is a source of incalculable strength."[38]

Finally, analogous to the vow of obedience is the acceptance of the leadership of the prior as servant of unity in the community. The rule exhorts the brothers to open fraternal relationships with the prior and to acceptance and collaboration in his ministry of leadership. "The prior appoints a brother to ensure continuity after him."[39] The second part of this section is an exhortation to the prior to look always to the good of the community and to avoid authoritarianism. This may be seen as an exhortation that Brother Roger addressed primarily to himself, as he was serving as prior at the time, and would continue to do so for over fifty years.

A section on brothers on mission contemplates a single unified community at Taizé in France, even when there are brothers serving in other places. It gives a few guidelines for brothers on mission, anticipating the time when small groups would live among the poor in many parts of the world. The brothers are to be "witnesses for Christ (and) a sign of his presence among all men and bearers of joy."[40] Over the decade the mission of the community has developed into an outreach to young adults who are yearning for spirituality and meaning, and who may or may not feel at home or fully nourished in their home churches.

Practical advice on new brothers provides that they are given time to adjust to the life of the Taizé community. New brothers are assigned to a brother who is charged to "listen to them and prepare them for profession."[41]

The rule ends with texts for the rite of profession of the brothers. The first is an exhortation to the brother to trust, vigilance, and joy. There follows a series of commitments of the new brother:

---

[38] *RT*, 31, 33.
[39] *RT*, 35.
[40] *RT*, 37.
[41] *RT*, 38.

Will you, for love of Christ, consecrate yourself to him with all your being? *I will.*

Will you, from now on, live out your call from God within our community, in communion with your brothers? *I will.*

Will you live with your brothers in the community of material and spiritual goods, which lies in all openness of heart? *I will.*

Will you, in order to be more available to serve with your brothers, and in order to give yourself in undivided love to Christ, remain celibate? *I will.*

Will you, so that we may be of one heart and one soul and so that our unity may be complete, accept the orientations of the community expressed by the servant of communion, remembering that he is only a poor man of the Gospel? *I will.*

Will you, always discerning Christ in your brothers, watch over them in good days and bad, in suffering and in joy? *I will.*

In consequence, on account of Christ and the Gospel, you are henceforth a brother of our community. May this ring be the sign of our faithfulness in the Lord.[42]

In the profession formula of the brothers of Taizé, it is easy to recognize the vows of religious life that are familiar in the Roman Catholic tradition.

The chapter on prayer gives attention to common prayer of the community, personal prayer, and the Eucharist. Times of prayer and ways of prayer are not presented, but the commitment to prayer is central. The common prayer of the Taizé community gradually evolved into the pattern of three daily times of prayer of the word of God, silence, often for long periods, and song—the music of Taizé is perhaps its most well-known fruit. Mercy and forgiveness form a synergy of love in community.

---

[42] *RT*, 44–45.

Brother Roger is very practical in discussing the realities of not liking each brother equally, the use of simple language ("no weak sentimentality, and no harsh words"), continual discussions which accomplish nothing, and the ministry of the prior in situations of conflict. Confession of sin to another brother (as also recommended by Bonhoeffer) is encouraged: "Confession is made to one and the same brother, chosen with the prior."[43]

Monastic life in all traditions has a leader, an abbot or abbess. In Taizé this is the prior who "inspires unity within the community."[44] He is first a servant and "his service is to stimulate the community, that microcosm of the Church entrusted to him, to strive for unanimity, to be of one soul."[45] He is one with his brothers as a real human being: "The prior is subject to the same failings as his brothers."[46] As so often happens with charismatic founders of communities, Brother Roger served in this ministry to the day of his death and designated Brother Alois Leser, a German Catholic, as his successor.

The rule of Taizé is brief and contains more exhortation and inspiration than prescription. Nevertheless, this rule definitely goes beyond the experiment of Bonhoeffer at Finkenwalde in its embrace of some aspects of religious life that had been rejected by the Reformation. Like Bonhoeffer, Brother Roger promotes the practice of common prayer, common life, and sharing goods. He also advocates confession of sins to another member of the community. However, unlike Bonhoeffer, he accepts the practice of celibacy and the permanent commitment to live in community under a prior. This moves the Taizé experience much closer to the traditional Catholic forms of religious life. Having existed for over fifty years, the lifestyle and spirituality of Taizé had more time to mature than Bonhoeffer

---

[43] *RT*, 27, 28.

[44] *RT*, 34.

[45] Roger Schutz. "L'Unamitie," in *An Ecumenical Light on the Renewal of Religious Community Life* (Pittsburgh, PA: Duquesne University Press, 1966), 90.

[46] *RT*, 34.

and his community at Finkenwalde. Brother Roger describes the experience this way:

> If there is such a thing as a spirituality of Taizé, it is nothing other than the wish to run according to the Pauline sense; to run together and not separately. This means abandoning a purely individualistic search for salvation to desire the salvation of all. This track takes us toward the finishing post, we can only run if we all gaze together on the Christ of glory.[47]

Reformers had rejected religious life because it seemed to be premised on two classes of Christians, the basic Christians, who were the people in the pews, and the religious, who were "Christians on steroids." Brother Roger felt the vocation to live the gospel deliberately and single-heartedly, a vocation he held in common with every Christian, as well as with generations of religious through the history of Christianity. He also gives important insights into the living of religious life in today's world, describing the Taizé experience as a parable of community. Taizé was not organized to do a particular work, though it has had a strong emphasis on service to the poor from the very beginning. The purpose of the community was none other than to come together and live the gospel in community, sharing prayer, community, and mission. This living parable of community is intended to balance the instinct to gather in community with a distinct internal cohesion, with the desire to remain in relationship with the wider Christian community, and at the service of this broader community.

Even before Bonhoeffer's community at Finkenwalde and Brother Roger's community at Taizé, Dorothy Day and her collaborators began the Catholic Worker movement in the United States. Day had strong communitarian instincts even before she converted to Catholicism, and although she had connections with men and women religious, she and her collaborators

---

[47] Schutz, *This Day Belongs to God*, 45.

established the Catholic Worker as a lay movement. The next section examines her life, and her autobiographical work *The Long Loneliness,* and the Catholic Worker movement.

DOROTHY DAY
AND THE CATHOLIC WORKER MOVEMENT

Dorothy Day (1897–1980) was born in Brooklyn, New York to Grace and John Day, who were nominal Episcopalians. Her father was a journalist, and the growing family moved to Oakland, where her father worked for a newspaper. Shortly after the earthquake of 1906, the family moved to Chicago, where Dorothy lived in her adolescent years. She attended the University of Illinois at Urbana-Champaign for two years. During this time she was increasingly interested in radical social movements and was particularly concerned with the plight of the poor and with workers. She did not complete her studies, but instead, went with her family when they moved back to New York in 1916. She began working as a journalist on *The Call,* a socialist newspaper in New York. This work allowed her to pursue her interests in the labor movement and participate in protests she was covering for the newspaper. She witnessed the increasing crackdowns on protesters firsthand, and she spent time in jail as a suffragist.[48] She continued writing for several socialist papers and eventually wrote a semi-autobiographical novel that gave her greater financial stability.

Dorothy bought a beach house on Staten Island, where she lived with Forster Batterham, her common-law husband. During this time she became increasingly interested in religion, an interest that caused conflict in her relationship with Batterham, whom she loved deeply. Batterham opposed marriage and also opposed all religion but shared her interest in social reform.

---

[48] Dorothy Day, *The Long Loneliness: The Autobiography of the Legendary Catholic Social Activist* (New York: HarperOne, 1996), 19–22, 36–50, 72–83. Cited hereafter as *LL.*

Dorothy became pregnant and resolved to have her child baptized Catholic, deepening the rift between the couple. Soon after her daughter, Tamar Theresa, was born in 1926, Dorothy had her baptized. After a difficult break with Batterham, Dorothy herself became Catholic the following year in Our Lady Help of Christians Parish on Staten Island. There followed a period of travel as she sought to distance herself from Batterham and to support herself and her daughter. She spent a short time in Hollywood as a screen writer, went on to Mexico, then returned to New York when her daughter became ill.[49]

In 1932, Dorothy met Peter Maurin (1877–1949), a French-born social activist. Peter was born in southern France, one of twenty-four children of a farming family. He had spent some years teaching as a Christian Brother before immigrating to Canada as a homesteader. Later, he worked as a laborer in various places in the United States before settling in New York where he worked as a French tutor.[50] Dorothy and Peter met through a mutual friend and immediately found a deep resonance between them and a desire to put some of their ideas into concrete action.

Within a year Dorothy and Peter began collaboration on a project that came to be the Catholic Worker movement. The movement traces its origins to May Day, 1933. On that day the first copy of the newspaper, *The Catholic Worker*, went on sale on the streets of New York City. By the end of the year the paper had a circulation of 100,000. Houses of hospitality were part of the initial ideas of Peter Maurin. They began as a solution to the practical necessity of housing a growing number of people involved in the movement. "We never had any money, and the cheapest, most practical way to take care of people was to rent some apartments and have someone do the cooking for the lot of us."[51] The project developed organically, rather than through any overarching plan. Dorothy describes it this way:

---

[49] *LL*, 120, 134, 148, 158.

[50] Arthur Sheehan, *Peter Maurin: Gay Believer* (Garden City, NY: Hanover House, 1959), 52–69, 205.

[51] *LL*, 182, 185.

> We were just sitting there talking when Peter
> Maurin came in.
> We were just sitting there talking when lines of
> people began to form, saying, "We need
> bread. . . . "
> We were just sitting there talking and people
> moved in on us. . . .
> It was as casual as all that, I often think. It just
> came about. It just happened.[52]

Houses of hospitality sprang up in various cities, some directly
related to the project of Dorothy and Peter. Others were formed
when people read about the movement in *The Catholic Worker*
and sought to organize their own houses of hospitality after that
model. This loose organization enabled the project to spread
rapidly in order to meet the pressing social needs of the day.
In addition to urban houses of hospitality, several farms were
established as "agronomic universities," as Peter Maurin termed
them. Having been raised on a farm in France, Peter believed
that the solution to many of society's ills was for people to return
to the land.

Peter Maurin gave a significant orientation to the movement
through his own efforts to impart his vision of "forming the
structure of the new society within the shell of the old,"[53] words
he borrowed from the constitution of the Industrial Workers of
the World (IWW), which was in decline by the time the Catholic Worker movement began.

The Catholic Worker movement had strong anarchist lean-
ings and an emphasis on decentralization; thus there is no particular source for the vision or goals of the movement. Instead,
it must be distilled from the history of the movement and the
writings of Peter Maurin, as well as Dorothy Day's writings,
which regularly appeared in *The Catholic Worker*. She also wrote
several books, including an autobiographical work entitled *The*

---

[52] *LL*, 285.
[53] *LL*, 196.

Long Loneliness, which traces her own spiritual journey and the beginnings of the Catholic Worker movement. In addition to the writings of these two pillars of the movement, generations of Catholic Workers have joined and given years and sometimes decades of their lives to it. There are currently over two hundred Catholic Worker communities listed in the Cahtolic Worker on-line directory, 90 percent of them in the United States. Workers continue to reflect on the program, gain fresh insights into it, and give fresh expression to its common themes.

One oft-repeated formulation of the Catholic Worker ideal is the promotion of cult, culture, and cultivation. Thus each of the Workers seeks to develop a personal spiritual life and to devote time to personal and community prayer. For Day, this was traditional Catholic worship along with prayer and periodic retreats. For modern Workers there is a variety of prayer styles; personal spirituality remains an important component of the movement.

The second aspect, culture, means attention to the life of the mind. The Catholic Worker movement was born in the conversations of friends as they explored radically living the gospel and serving the pressing social needs of their day. Peter Maurin often gave lectures to whoever would listen, and the Catholic Workers also encouraged regular conversation about important aspects of the community's life together. These gatherings, called round tables for clarification of thought, invited workers, volunteers, and others associated with the community to give voice to their convictions and to listen to the convictions of others. These conversations helped to stimulate a deepening of the values held in common. There was no effort to persuade, only an opportunity to explore a topic of common interest in order to deepen each person's understanding, renew his or her commitment, and gather fresh insight.

Finally, cultivation was seen as an integral part of the Catholic Worker program. In the early years Day, Maurin, and other workers began several farming communities. Some met with moderate success, but most were eventually abandoned. "One of the main difficulties of all these farm ventures is the lack of skills, money and equipment; lack of leadership too is a factor."[54]

The Catholic Worker movement continues to found communities of hospitality, attempting to create a society where it is easier to be good—places where gospel values are deliberately and systematically integrated into the life of the community through personal commitment and regular clarification of thought and values. At the end of *The Long Loneliness* Day names three "most significant" things:

> The most significant thing about *The Catholic Worker* is poverty, some say.
> The most significant thing is community, others say. We are not alone any more.
> But the final word is love.[55]

These three elements, voluntary poverty, community, and love are important to understanding the Catholic Worker movement and its importance in a theology of community. Each requires exploration.

Voluntary poverty is a liberating choice to step out of what Dorothy named in a 1956 *Catholic Worker* article the "rotten, decadent, putrid industrial capitalist system." Poverty is a choice to forgo accumulating luxuries in order to have enough of the essentials for everyone and to have more to share with those in need. This is not the same as *destitution*, which is a cruel and demeaning form of poverty. Catholic Workers acknowledge only those privileged with a certain financial stability are able to choose voluntary poverty. Many do not choose poverty, poverty chooses them. It is their fate because they have fallen victim to the many injustices of today's system. Voluntary poverty is a choice of those with enough economic security to make this choice. They make it because they find they can live richer and

---

[54] *LL*, 234.
[55] *LL*, 285.

fuller lives by serving the poor and witnessing to the wider society to the values of simplicity, sustainability, and solidarity with the poor.

Community is also at the heart of the Catholic Worker project. After becoming Catholic, Day never wanted to be called a communist or socialist because these two movements were condemned by the Catholic Church. She preferred the term *communitarian*, and she embraced the term *anarchist* as the style of community government. She saw her communitarianism as distinct from the collectivism found in communist or socialist systems because of her strong emphasis on the dignity of the person. Each person, no matter how poor, how sick, or how weak was created and loved by God. She identified in a deeply personal way with laborers, single mothers, the homeless, the addicted, and each of those who came looking for bread and soup. Dorothy's was a personalist communitarianism that sought to balance the needs of the individual and the community. The community's needs were important because of the individuals in the community. In the great dialectic of her day, capitalism versus communism, she sought to integrate the individual orientation of capitalism with the social orientation of communism.

The Catholic Worker movement went beyond collective living, motivated by economic and practical reasons. It was able to form communities because of the emphasis on the importance of the person in community. Each person possessed a dignity based on his or her creation in the image of God, a God who is Love. Possessing this innate dignity, each person deserved the respect of each other person in community. In addition, each person should have the opportunity for personal development, even while working hard to alleviate the sufferings of his or her brothers and sisters. Catholic Worker communities struggle to attain a balance among these values: personal rootedness, community commitment, and outreach to the poor.[56] The openness

---

[56] Carolyn Griffeth, "A Model for Building the Beloved Community for Catholic Workers and Fellow Travelers," *The RoundTable* (Summer 2012): 4–6.

to the process of clarification of thought is an important tool in striking this balance on an ongoing basis.

Finally, Day says that the final word is love, the love of God, who creates us in love, in the image of divine love. We find ourselves in loving God, and we learn to love by surrendering to the love of God, which is beyond all measure. We turn to others in community in love where we are challenged and supported in our God-quest. Together, then, we turn to our neighbors in service, particularly toward the weakest and most vulnerable among them.

The Catholic Worker orientation in community seeks to strike the balance between the individual and that community that some religious communities lost, particularly in the great collective houses of the early to mid-twentieth century. While Catholic Workers believe passionately in individual freedom, in contrast, in religious communities "the task determined the community."[57] Communities of religious women, in the great expansion in the middle of the twentieth century, could sometimes become impersonal collectivities where individual needs were sacrificed to the project of the group, and sometimes they were sacrificed to ministerial projects even at the expense of the group itself. The renewal movements of Vatican II sought a corrective for this reality, regaining the focus on the person, sometimes at the expense of community.

The Catholic Worker is a movement, not an organization. Finkenwalde and Taizé were organizations, the one a seminary, and the other an ecumenical community. Bonhoeffer did not write in detail about the authority structures in *Life Together,* and this is likely the case because the community at Finkenwalde gathered in the context of seminary education, which had its own structures of authority. The rule of Taizé does speak about authority structures. The principal structure of authority is the council of brothers, which includes all professed brothers of the community. The prior presides over the council and is the

---

[57] Dennis J. Geaney, *The Quest for Community: Tomorrow's Parish Today* (Notre Dame, IN: Ave Maria Press, 1987), 123–24.

servant of unity rather than the overlord of the community. The Catholic Worker takes this notion of authority and moves it a little further along the anarchist scale. "Anarchists believe that the whole people composing a community should take care of what governing is to be done, rather than have a distant and centralized State do it."[58] This anarchist orientation allows each Catholic Worker community to develop its own way of living the ideal of the movement. Small self-organizing communities are networked among themselves for mutual support. Each local community builds its network of supporters and volunteers who wish to share and live the values even if they are not living in the community.

Our final witness to community is Jean Vanier who began his work in community in the later twentieth century, when Taizé and the Catholic Worker were already well under way. He is the only writer we are examining who comes from a Catholic background. He sought to build a particular type of community as a lay movement with deep spiritual and humanitarian roots.

JEAN VANIER AND L'ARCHE

Jean Vanier was born in 1928 in Geneva, the son of the nineteenth governor general of Canada, who was in the diplomatic service in Switzerland at the time. After a period of service in the Navy during World War II, Vanier studied theology and philosophy in Paris and then taught philosophy at the University of St. Michael's College, University of Toronto. In 1964, Vanier welcomed two mentally handicapped men into his home to form community with them. This began a lifelong process of self-discovery and personal growth for Vanier. It was also the beginning of the L'Arche movement, in which mentally handicapped people form community with assistants. Vanier believed that communities committed to gospel living could be the leaven so needed by our society.

---

[58] *LL*, 268.

So many in our world today are suffering from isolation, war, and oppression. So much money is spent on the construction of armaments. Many, many young people are in despair because of the danger of nuclear war. Today as never before we need communities of welcome, communities that are a sign of peace in a world of war.[59]

Jean Vanier's thought and reflections on his experiences in community are found in a variety of writings and presentations over the decades since the founding of L'Arche. One of the principal, focused resources on the topic of community is the book *Community and Growth*, first published in French in 1979 with the title *La Communauté: Lieu du Pardon et de la Fête.* The book was written fifteen years after the beginning of the L'Arche experiment and was revised in 1989, after another ten years of life and reflection by Vanier. It includes his response to the critique of the original edition.

This book provides a wealth of insight and valuable reflection on the experience of living community. It describes the desire for community and societal factors that affect this desire and the assumptions and brokenness of those who come to community. This section examines some of Vanier's key insights that contribute to developing a theology of community.

In the introduction Vanier points out that our society today has particular features that make founding communities both more necessary and more difficult. In the past, societies were more homogeneous and cohesive, whether based on family, tribe, or populations that lived in the same town or village for generations. These cultures had a high sense of collectivity and mutual support. While this could lend itself to a sense of community, it could also keep people in bonds of fear and social pressures. By contrast, cultures in modern Western democracies are diverse and mobile, leading to a greater sense of individuality, which can also keep people in bonds of fear and social pressures. This leads to a "stark individualism" and thus

---

a greater loneliness; ironically, it also leads to a greater desire for community.[60]

The second half of the twentieth century saw significant developments in society. The 1960s and 1970s were an expansive time, as large cohorts of idealistic young people sought to throw away the old and build something new. This shifted by the 1980s and 1990s, when the generations coming of age were disillusioned by the generation that came before them. They saw social problems as being too big to solve, and many became apathetic and sought escape. Those who still sought to take on the challenges of society were drawn to create or join communities. These were occasionally misguided attempts to drown personal loneliness in community. But some also had the insights to build true community. They sought to "integrate the vision into their own hearts and minds and to develop their own inner freedom and choices, learning little by little to be led inwardly by love, rather than from the outside, by rigid laws."[61] Vanier had high hopes for these communities, especially when they were faith based:

> If, however, their religious faith opens up, on the one hand to the mystical—that is, to an experience of the love of God present in the community and in the heart of each person—and, on the other hand, to what unifies all human beings, especially the poor, the vulnerable and the oppressed, they will then continue to grow in openness.[62]

These communities develop a deep faith and engage "poverty, insecurity, and vulnerability" on many levels. For Vanier, poverty, insecurity, and vulnerability are outwardly manifest in the handicapped individuals who are the center of the L'Arche communities. However, he quickly discovered that forming community with the mentally handicapped made him much

---

[60] *C&G*, 1–3, 15.
[61] *C&G*, 4–5.
[62] *C&G*, 7.

more aware of his own personal poverty, insecurity, and vulnerability. He had to engage his own "monsters" on a personal and spiritual level as well as on a community level.[63] People would rather leave these things hidden and engage from a position of strength; however, true community forms when they are able to engage with the full truth of who they are, freeing untapped energies and strengths.

> When I use the word "community" in this book, I am talking essentially of groupings of people who have left their own milieu to live with others under the same roof, and work from a new vision of human beings and their relationships with each other and with God. . . . [Community is not] simply gathering together under the same roof a few people who get on reasonably well together or who are committed to the same ideal.[64]

Nor is community a mere matter of finding the perfect structure. A group must gather, common ideals are helpful, some insight into structure and organization is essential, but there is more needed than these fundamental ingredients for the building of a good community.

Vanier explores the elements that are needed for good community in a chapter entitled "One Heart, One Soul, One Spirit." A community is a place where a group of people can put down roots, or as Vanier says, they are "earthed." They begin to build a common identity as well as finding a space to enter into relationship. "Love is what we most want, yet it is what we fear the most," because love makes us vulnerable and open. As people are left free to develop their personal spirituality, they are more able to open themselves to the group and engage it. However, as each member does this, the group is always growing and changing. Thus this very openness is the strength and weakness of community. "There is nothing stronger than a heart which loves

---

[63] C&G, 8–9.
[64] C&G, 10–12.

and is freely given to God and to others." Strong communities are built of strong individuals. In a community it is important to balance the sense of self and the sense of the group; growth in personal identity can help in the growth of a group identity. Likewise, there must be a sense of personal boundaries and personal openness. It is not healthy to be completely open at all times. In the same way, it is important to establish community boundaries as well as a sense of hospitality and of openness to those outside the group. Vanier says, quoting Bonhoeffer: "He who loves community, destroys community; he who loves the brethren, builds community."[65]

Freedom and Commitment

It is also important to balance freedom and commitment. Individuals should freely engage in community and embrace its values. This is consistent with the decision to make a commitment to the community whether temporary or long term. Freedom allows each person to grow in his or her commitment, and even to grow apart from the community's vision. At the same time, in order for the community to grow, each member must be willing to surrender some individual freedom to the group.

> Some out of fear of this conflict and of loneliness will refuse to follow their personal freedom and inner conscience; they choose not to 'rock the boat.' Others will choose to grow personally but the price they will have to pay will be a certain anguish and loneliness as they feel separated from the group. . . . The loneliness and anguish felt by this person can lead to a more intimate and mystical union with God.[66]

Thus each person is free to come and commit to the group. The members of a group support one another's commitment

---

[65] *C&G*, 14, 22, 22.

[66] *C&G*, 24.

and freedom. This is a challenge, but a community can only grow if its members grow. At the same time, interdependence is important to build a greater sense of community, and this grows with trust. In addition, this frees each person to grow in personal spirituality.

> In each person's heart of hearts there is also the deep and secret union with God, the Bridegroom, which corresponds to their secret and eternal name. . . . . Community is the safe place where all of us feel free to be ourselves.[67]

The community's rules and structures are an embodiment of the community's values. They enable the group to move forward with some predictability and without calling a community meeting every time a decision is needed. Yet "community is a place for people and for their growth, before being a place of laws and rules."[68] Brother Roger noted in his rule that excessive rules can be a substitute for living in freedom and responsibility with daily openness and discernment. For both writers it is not a question of either freedom or rules. Instead, writing in the mid-twentieth century, they call their followers to greater personal responsibility and freedom, cautioning them against overreliance on rules and structures.

Called

In view of the personal challenge of living in community and balancing personal and group needs for freedom and mutual commitment, Vanier reminds us that the sense of a call can be a powerful bond among community members. "We are called to this by God who gives the grace."[69] Each of the authors we have examined would agree with Vanier on this point. However, the call they name is not external to oneself—an objective call from

---

[67] C&G, 54.

[68] C&G, 56.

[69] C&G, 45.

a distant divinity. Instead, it is an inner bond, being true to the God-image in which they were created that desires community. Those who have just arrived come because they find the community as it exists resonates with their own desires. After being drawn by this resonance, those who give their lives to the community speak their deepest truth into the circle of trust formed by the community and listen deeply to the truth of others. This truth is spoken in times of community discussion and, more important, is lived in the day-to-day actions and decisions of the community. Vanier quotes Henri J. M. Nouwen in support of this understanding of the call to community as a response to each one's deepest truth:

> We were together before we came together. . . . Community life is not a creation of human will but an obedient response to the reality of our being united. Many people who lived together for years and whose love for one another has been tested more than once know that the decisive experience in their life was not that they were able to hold together but that they were held together.[70]

In addition to the first call or first attraction to community "to do wonderful and noble things," Vanier speaks of a second call. This second call has a realism born of experience when "we accept that we cannot do big or heroic things."[71] This is the time when community members begin to put down roots and do the hard work of commitment and begin to find the more abundant blessings of community, both for themselves and for others. Bonhoeffer also realized this when he described the personal growth that was necessary before someone could begin to preach credibly and fruitfully.

Vanier realizes that many people come to community out of their own personal needs. He calls this "community for myself."

---

[70] *C&G*, 45–46, quoting Henri J. M. Nouwen, "Solitude and Community," *Worship* 52, no. 1 (January 1978): 18.

[71] *C&G*, 139.

This is not a bad place to begin, but it can be damaging if each one remains only for his or her own needs, even an altruistic need to serve. A community that is growing "is a place where everyone—or, let's be realistic, the majority!—is emerging from the shadows of egocentricity to the light of a real love." It takes time for members to grow beyond "community for me" to "me for community," in which I am able to surrender my own needs and desires to the needs and desires of the group. As one moves from "I" to "we," the "I" does not ever disappear. In part it remains an "I" as the person grows, and in part it is incorporated into the "we" of community, both contributing to the growth of the community and surrendering or accommodating to the needs and vision of the community. In the end, the growing "we" of community reaches beyond itself and becomes community for God and others, without ever losing the personal or community identity.[72]

Life of the Community

After looking at the place of the individual in community, Vanier turns to the life of the community. Some, particularly the young, come to the community as a place to deepen their spirituality, grow in personal maturity, and give themselves in service. After a time they move on, though they often maintain a connection to the community and carry its values with them throughout their lives. Others put down roots, spending decades or even a lifetime in the community. These people are important to any community movement since they give it stability and longevity. Their long-term commitment can help the community to sustain those who stay for just a few months or years. The needs of these two types of members are different, as is their orientation. Both are important to the longevity of L'Arche and other community movements. Over time, the community learns to negotiate these differences in a way that fosters the growth and freedom of all.

---

[72] *C&G*, 55, 57.

It is also important that a community find ways of speaking honestly when there are differences, conflicts, and even individuals who are destructive to the life of the community. For some today, the ability to live in community cannot be assumed. "Only the people with responsibility in the community and its long-term members can decide that someone must go. But in doing this, they too must recognize their share of guilt."[73] It is unrealistic to think that conflicts will never arise or that individuals will never become destructive. Here Vanier is quick to point out that when they do arise, we all do well to name our own share of guilt in allowing a situation to get out of hand. He calls the long-term members to a special role in this, because they have a greater experience and responsibility for the tenor of life in community.

> A hundred years ago it was not too large a leap for many to make the passage from family life, with its rhythm, structures of obedience and traditional values, to the life of a religious community. Today that leap is immense. For today people have been nourished on independence and individualism, the desire to win and go up the ladder. . . . Communities need to learn how to welcome those who have succeeded in the world and to give them the right support so they can climb down the ladder into the place of communion.[74]

Those who come to community will need time to make the transition from independence to interdependence and mutual responsibility. Just as it takes a community time to form and negotiate this relationship, each new member who comes to community will go through a period of arrival, disillusionment, adjustment, and finally a measure of stability. It can help new members if the community is "upfront about its fundamental

---

[73] C&G, 127.
[74] C&G, 76.

attitudes toward money, sex and power, rights and obligations, trial period and accompaniment."[75]

The community also has to be attentive to boundaries: "A community has to be apart from society and open to it at the same time." A community comes together because of specific shared values that are distinct from the dominant culture: justice, sustainability, spirituality, service. If it did not have a distinct identity, it would not need to gather. Thus, it has to take a step apart from society, yet if it does not remain in relationship with society, it can close in on itself and lose its evangelical sharpness. Vanier is clear about the high ideals of community and the downward trend of those ideals over time: "Communities start in mystery and end in bureaucracy."[76] It takes the conscious efforts of all to continue to renew itself, its members and its mission.

Vanier reflects on community as a philosopher with years of experience in human behavior. The unique orientation of L'Arche, forming community with those with mental handicaps, gives him a unique perspective from which to explore the meaning and types of strength and weakness. From this perspective he brings important insights to a theology of community.

COMMON THREADS

Each of the writers we have examined had his or her own particular genius and insight. They also share many elements in common. Bonhoeffer tried to strike the balance between solitude and life in community for the seminarians struggling to be true to gospel values in the heart of Nazi Germany. Dorothy Day also tried to strike this balance, based on a strong sense of personalism, which meant, according to Brigid O'Shea Merriman, that she "recognized the dignity of the human person

---

[75] *C&G*, 79.
[76] *C&G*, 127, 110.

both as an individual and as a participant member of human society."[77] She agreed with much of the communist and socialist critique of capitalism, but she preferred to call her movement communitarian because, unlike those two collectivist movements, she strongly valued the human person, made in the image of God. Because Vanier's movement envisions communities of people with and without intellectual disabilities, his writing explores the paradox of strength and weakness in community. His approach is philosophical and psychological as he reflects on the realities of building community. Brother Roger brings the special lens of ecumenism to his work on community, focusing on the values that unite rather than particular beliefs and practices that divide the Christian community. His community has become a center of pilgrimage for the young who are seeking spiritual meaning in today's world.

In addition to their unique perspectives, the four writers we have examined have a number of common threads as they attempt to build Christian community in today's world. In some ways they each take elements of community that are the stock in trade of religious life over the centuries. In drawing together the common threads, it is interesting to observe the elements that they have in common with that great legacy and those elements that they leave behind. We examine this in three main areas: spirituality, mission, and community. Of these, there are definite changes in the notions of spirituality and mission, but most significant innovations are in the way that community is envisioned.

Spirituality

All of the writers and movements hold prayer and spirituality to be central. Liturgical prayer in common was an important part of the life that they proposed. It is fair to say that the successors of Bonhoeffer and Dorothy Day in the New Monasticism and Catholic Worker are less strident in their commitment to

---

[77] Brigid O'Shea Merriman, *Searching for Christ: The Spirituality of Dorothy Day* (Notre Dame, IN: University of Notre Dame Press, 1994), 53.

liturgical prayer, but it is still valued within those movements. Liturgical prayer at the community at Taizé attracts pilgrims from around the globe and is imitated in local Taizé prayer services in various places. Over all, the common prayer in these movements has shifted away from timeless, unchanging ritual and opened up to more spontaneity and to more silence.

All of the writers and movements value personal spirituality and solitude to a greater degree than the traditions from which they come. Bonhoeffer stressed the importance of times of solitude and private prayer as essential to an individual having the capacity to come into community and to engage in common prayer. However, Bonhoeffer describes personal prayer as a time dedicated to "meditation on the Scripture, prayer and intercession." He specifically warns against straying into "self-indulgent rumination" and even against deeper forms of quiet prayer.[78]

The rule of Taizé is explicit in its call to solitude and inner stillness as a place of intimate encounter with God. Both Dorothy Day and Jean Vanier speak of the necessity of deep personal relationship with God nourished in times of solitude and personal prayer. A contemplative dimension is essential to life in community and to the strong commitment to mission that are at the heart of their movements.

All four writers and movements have a definite shift in the balance of prayer to the personal responsibility and spirituality of the individual in community. It is not enough to participate in the rituals of the community; each person must commit to "a disciplined contemplative life."[79]

Mission

Like spirituality, mission has been a central element of religious life for most of its history and in most of its manifestations. Even contemplatives have a missionary aspect as they support others

---

[78] *LT*, 86.

[79] Rutba House, ed., *School(s) for Conversion: Twelve Marks of a New Monasticism* (Eugene, OR: Wipf & Stock Publishers, 2005), 162.

in prayer and witness as well as providing places of refuge and retreat to their more active brothers and sisters. Often new religious communities have gathered to meet unmet needs in their particular time and place. In twentieth-century America the ministries of many religious communities were overwhelmingly focused on education and healthcare. Often hospitals and schools were established to meet unmet needs, but over time they have found themselves in increasingly competitive fields, crowded with others seeking to serve those same needs. In response, some institutional ministries have excelled in a particular aspect of education or healthcare services, while others have closed. This has enabled religious to turn their energies to other unmet needs.

The outreach of Catholic Worker, New Monastics, Taizé, and L'Arche has been able to focus on the new needs of our day, service to the poor and marginalized, justice and sustainability. They do evangelization not so much by words as through the witness of their lives and ministry and through sharing faith among themselves and with guests, volunteers, and others who sojourn with them in community and ministry. They are not tied to large institutional ministries but have been freer to meet these needs in a small, local way. None of them seeks to solve all the world's problems; rather, they seek to provide a model for a more just and sustainable society while meeting the urgent needs of a few people in their neighborhood. In addition, they often choose neighborhoods that are more marginalized in order to be of service where the need is great. These movements are not in the business of building large institutions. Instead, they are leaven in their local neighborhoods and find support in their network of communities. In this way any one of the movements is greater than the sum of its parts and is able to provide support to communities in the network and to help to increase the service they are able to bring.

Community

The greatest innovations in these movements are, not surprisingly, the way they organize themselves in community. All four writers and the movements they inspired saw community as a central need both in the church and in society, plagued as they are by growing individualism and increasing fragmentation. In religious life men and women have generally lived in communities whose general framework has been framed by vowed life and commitment to mission. Members were vowed to celibacy, shared goods in common, and were committed to decision making in community. The culture and spirituality around sharing of goods and shared decision making varied widely from one tradition to another, for example, Benedictine or Franciscan, as well as in different times and places in one tradition.

Postmodern society is marked by "the emergence of individualism and the consequent collapse of the sense of community."[80] Parker Palmer observes that "we have been drawn toward cities large and complicated enough to meet our economic desires and toward families small and portable (and even disposable) enough to make mobility possible." This movement is not without its cost: with the breakdown of the common life there can come a growing sense of personal disintegration.[81]

Some feel this collapse of a sense of community particularly keenly and turn to the various communitarian movements that are developing in our society in order to find again that sense of community. However, they come at community from a different place. Eschewing meta-narratives or supreme models, postmoderns recognize the rich variety of micro-narratives of small local groups and societies. The communities of the New Monasticism, L'Arche, Catholic Worker, and Taizé and countless eco-villages and peace communities share a common story, though each tells it with different accents and emphases.

These communities begin when a small group gathers and networks with other communities, of both like and unlike. The

---

[80] Max Charlesworth, "Postmodernism and Theology," *The Way* 36, no. 3 (July 1996): 190.

[81] Parker J. Palmer, *The Promise of Paradox* (Notre Dame, IN: Ave Maria Press, 1980), 69, 70.

local Catholic Worker house is networked with other Catholic Worker houses across the country, but it is also networked with the local urban farming community, religious communities, and other intentional communities in the area. Communities gather to "comfort and confront."[82] They seek to give comfort to their members who are then "no longer alone."[83] They also seek to comfort their neighbor, particularly the poor and the marginalized, as they reach out to them in mission and human solidarity. In addition, they confront their members, challenging one another to grow in personal integrity, authenticity, and service. At the same time they confront unjust and unsustainable systems in society. While they seek to comfort the most vulnerable, they also seek to confront the systems that oppress them, and they call the vulnerable to be all that they can be, despite injustices and obstacles, and walk with them on this journey.

Several of the writers explore the importance of personal freedom and responsibility in community, seeking to strike a different balance between the individual and the group. Only when each member is freely committing to a personal spirituality and to working for justice can the group come together in mutual strength and respect. Dorothy Day saw personalism as a counterbalance to the dehumanizing collectivism found in communism and even in some religious communities. Bonhoeffer's much quoted phrase also points to this reality: "Let him who cannot be alone beware of community . . . let him who is not in community beware of being alone."[84] Vanier believes that each person has a unique gift to bring to community, and that gift can only be liberated and shared when all persons are free to be themselves.

This emphasis on the freedom and responsibility of each individual affects the form of leadership found in these community movements. Obedience in religious communities has had many interpretations over time. At root, it is a commitment to listen to the voice of God found in scripture, leaders, and the

---

[82] Geaney, *The Quest for Community*, 9, 11.

[83] *LL*, 285; see also *RT*, 83.

[84] *LT*, 81, 83.

gathered community. At times it is an opening to collaborative discernment among brothers and sisters in community or in chapter. The level of personal responsibility that is encouraged or allowed has also varied over time. Current canon law describes it this way:

> The evangelical counsel of obedience, undertaken in the spirit of faith and love in the following of Christ, who was obedient even unto death, obliges submission of one's will to lawful Superiors, who act in the place of God when they give commands that are in accordance with each institute's own constitutions. (canon 601)

None of the four writers discussed, or their followers, would be comfortable with submission of will to one acting in the place of God. They all recognize a need to open one's heart and mind to others in the discernment process, but they place a high value on personal freedom and responsibility before God. For this reason the community gathered in discernment is the focal point of leadership. One who holds an office in the community has the responsibility of fostering consensus and discernment. The prior of Taizé is probably the strongest leader figure in the movements described, and he is described as the servant of communion, not the representative of God in the community. Bonhoeffer's brief experiment at Finkenwalde was lived out within the hierarchy of the seminary, but the New Monastics who follow his inspiration generally follow an egalitarian style of community. Catholic Workers follow Dorothy Day, who subscribes to anarchy as a form of government in which all decisions are made by those who are affected by the decision. This idea is not new; it conforms to a maxim of medieval canon law: *quod omnes tangit ab omnibus approbari debet* (what touches all should be approved by all). This maxim describes the democratic self-government that has characterized some religious communities over the course of history, as members gathered in chapter to discuss and decide weightier matters of the life of the community.

Another area in which the writers converge is the topic of boundaries. The community has to strike a balance between boundaries and openness to the wider society. In community there is an important relationship between boundaries and identity. If the boundaries are too permeable, then the identity of the individual and of the community becomes blurred. Some internal space is necessary. There is also a relationship between inclusivity and sustainability. Inclusivity is a high value for communities, and it is sometimes difficult to set up boundaries. However, intentional communities have learned by experience that if everyone is included, the vision of the group is dissipated and community is unsustainable. Some communities choose to be inclusive at the expense of sustainability; as the group eventually disperses, other communities may form. Communities that desire long-term sustainability learn to negotiate the balance between inclusiveness and boundaries. Often there will be layers of community, or a community of communities. This allows each person to choose a level of commitment and involvement. Those who are long-term, live-in members have a greater commitment to the community and a greater voice in important decisions. Those who choose a short-term or limited commitment have a more limited voice in decisions of the community.

Bonhoeffer's original experiment at Finkenwalde was short term because it was a seminary. Taizé is a more long-term commitment, inviting brothers to make a life-time commitment in community after a period of formation. Catholic Worker and L'Arche have both short-term and long-term members, as do the communities in the New Monasticism movement. These groups have come to an understanding of the balance between the levels of commitment. It can be a great part of the community's purpose to give space to young people to experience this type of Christian community for a time while choosing their path in life. It can be a place of growth and maturation for them, and they bring energy and vitality to the community and to its mission. Some of these members will put down roots in the community and become the next generation of long-term members.

These four writers and the communities that they gathered and described are evolving a form of community that is similar to that which religious communities have lived over the centuries. They also have some distinct differences that we examine in the coming chapters. Many of the men and women who are seeking religious life today long for communities that exemplify a radical commitment to shared gospel living and to a balanced and humane lifestyle where there is time for prayer, community, and mission. They seek to incarnate the gospel here and now, asking what task God might take up on moving into our neighborhood. In small local communities they become peacemakers, share the good news, live lightly on the earth, and actively pursue justice. They share life, goods, and spirituality, and they can support one another in the commitments they have made.

CHAPTER THREE

SEEDS OF NEWNESS

We turn now to explore the current place of religious life and seek to discover the seeds of newness in this situation. There are three thousand religious women under the age of fifty-five in the United States; these women are in 450 different institutes, leaving just a handful in most institutes.[1] What is this about? Wouldn't good planning, efficiency, and sustainability require that these women be concentrated in fewer communities, so that they would be able to support one another and there would be a few sustainable communities? Or is there something else afoot here? What is the Spirit's call in this context? Is it possible to discover God's plan, God's dream for the future of religious life in the seeds of newness today?

Speaking with the women in the minority cohort in religious life, I find a few hints about the dream of God for the future. These are really amazing women; they are confident, articulate leaders, yet they are so few in their communities that their voices and insights can be lost. The unique voice and perspective they bring has not yet gained a significant hearing in the wider reality of religious life. Like any other cultural minority, it is only with difficulty that the dominant culture can actually hear and understand the voices of younger women religious on their own terms. Often newer members find themselves translating and explaining, rather than speaking their own truth in its own native language. Too often, rather than gaining momentum, these voices, when they are heard, echo around a bit, then fade

---

[1] *NRRO Annual Report* (Washington DC: National Religious Retirement Office, 2011).

away. While this can be a frustrating experience for the minority cohort, I believe it is as it should be. The dominant cohort has an important task in bringing to completion its work of renewal. The minority cohort has another task, and it is a task that is the work of the few, not the many. All of us in religious life today will have to summon our courage to engage the challenges ahead and set out steadfastly on paths yet untrodden.

Some sociologists have said that between 75 percent and 90 percent of religious communities in existence in the United States today are currently in their last generation.[2] One of the primary factors to be considered in assessing the viability of a religious institute is demographics; for example, more than half of the members are in retirement or semi-retirement. While these members continue to be active well into their seventies and eighties, this factor negatively affects the viability of the group. The institute relies increasingly on its investments and pensions, rather than income from active members. Fewer and fewer new members come to join the group, and because of the widening age gap, they find it more and more difficult to integrate socially and culturally into the community. Change in these institutes generally means selling properties that have played a significant role in the life of the community, for example, the motherhouse. It also means relinquishing control and many of the ongoing ties with important ministries and other partners. All these are signs that "what is" is passing away. While some interpret this as failure and defeat, it may be more accurately seen as the natural evolution of a particular cohort in religious life. One of its tasks was to build the Catholic education and healthcare systems. Another of these tasks was to empower the laity to take its place in the mission of Jesus carried out in these apostolic works. Having built the institutes and empowered lay ministers, older members can take a rightful pride in the implementation of a key component of the renewal sought by the Second Vatican Council. Not only

---

[2] Diarmuid O'Murchu, *Consecrated Religious Life: The Changing Paradigms* (Maryknoll, NY: Orbis Books, 2005).

have they renewed religious life, but they also have been key players in the renewal in the church at large and in enabling lay ministry in an unprecedented way in their own institutions.

What is, is passing away. The dominant cohort in religious life today can hold its head high, knowing its members have done amazing things in their ministries and institutions, as well as in building up the people of God. They have taught and healed generations of the weakest and most vulnerable. They are in the process of writing their last chapters, both individually and corporately. As in any good book, the last chapter is the culmination of all that has come before, and is often the best and most satisfying to read. No one wants a good book to come to an end. But end it must, and blessed are those whose privilege it is to write that chapter.

Some newer members from the midst of these communities are eager to be set free to begin writing the sequel with their lives. The minority cohort is also distinct in its strong intercommunity relationships, supports, and sensibilities. In the days before, during, and shortly after Vatican II, men and women entered religious life in large groups, as we have discussed. Often they came from schools and colleges sponsored by the community they entered. They spent their early years in their community's formation programs with other members of the same community. During this time, their ties with family and friends were limited as were those with other men and women religious. Often even their academic work was done in institutions of their own congregation, where their contacts with others outside the community were limited. In contrast, women of the minority cohort have been involved in intercommunity programs from the beginning of their religious lives, and they maintain strong relationship with religious in other institutes.[3]

Men and women considering religious life today have had little contact with religious in their schools, colleges, parishes,

---

[3] *Author's note*—If you are a woman religious in this cohort, I urge you to connect with giving-voice.org or contact me and I'll help you plug in to the networks and conversations.

and workplaces. They often contact several communities and may participate in vocation discernment programs that are jointly sponsored by several religious institutes. Once they enter, they maintain a strong social network with family and friends as they begin to integrate their lives into the communities they are entering. From their earliest days of formation they connect with religious of other communities. This happens in intercommunity formation programs where communities in a given geographic region or charismatic grouping[4] pool their resources to provide classes and workshops of religious life, theology, human and spiritual development, and so on. Members also see collaboration in ministry settings where they might work in a co-sponsored ministry or another setting in which religious from various communities are involved. Inter-institute collaboration also occurs at social events, workshops, and retreats. Young religious today have a balance of experiences both within their own institute and among many institutes.

I propose that these facts give us a glimpse of God's dream. Martin Luther King, Jr.'s, famous speech had the refrain "I have a dream." In it, he laid out a future that his contemporaries could not imagine, but which, once articulated, found resonance with them, and was a source of the godly energy needed to make the dream a reality. I suggest that God, too, has a dream. God's dream for religious life in the United States is a dream bigger than those who are living the life right now, a dream bigger than any of their congregations, a dream the size of God, more than they can ask or imagine (see Eph 3:20). I believe this dream centers around several important elements: charism, community, connectivity, consciousness, and contemplation.

Charism is the deep story of each religious congregation, the story of what was done, but the more important story of

---

[4] Many religious institutes of women form national collaborative formation programs along charismatic lines, for example, Franciscan Common Novitiate, the Dominican Collaborative Novitiate, and the St. Joseph Federation Novitiate. These programs supplement the formation received in a new member's home congregation or province.

why it was done, and why it was done in the particular way it was done. The charism of an institute is that particular insight into living the gospel that inspires and impels each succeeding generation of a particular community to live as Franciscans or Dominicans or Mercies. This story resonates with the personal vocation of the individual members and their personal spirituality and helps to shape it. And together with their sisters, they reinterpret the life for a new generation, for a new place, and for a new cultural situation. And so they write new chapters of their story with their lives.

Newer members of these various communities are in a position to hear the founding stories, to breathe in the spirit, and to live the spirituality of the institutes. They gather the riches of each of their congregations as they nurture their own life, spirituality, and ministry. They do this even as the new is emerging and unfolding within and among them. In a slightly awkward metaphor, they take on the DNA of the charisms so that they can carry it forth into the heart of the twenty-first century, blessing those who have shared it with them so generously.

Community is an imperative element of the dream; it is a sign of our times. Individuals, families, and whole societies are feeling the fragmentation of modern living, and many cultural thinkers and spiritual writers are telling us that the healing of our personal and global spirits will happen through community or it will not happen at all.[5]

Connectivity is an important element of the dream. Religious of the future will not build institutions but webs, not mega-communities but small local communities in relationship, like the communities of Catholic Workers and L'Arche discussed in Chapter 2. So many of the most influential movements in the new consciousness are small networked organizations. This is the genius of the Occupy movement, of the peace movement, and of the Arab Spring.

New consciousness is an important element of the dream. Our world is becoming increasingly conscious of itself as a

---

[5] Dietrich Bonhoeffer, *Life Together* (New York: Harper and Row, 1954).

global, connected reality in which the good of one is intimately connected to the good of all. Moving forward, religious life must take stock of how it can live and contribute to this evolving consciousness.

Contemplation is the final element of the dream. The late twentieth and early twenty-first centuries have seen a flourishing interest in spirituality, even while it has seen a waning interest in organized religion. And within organized religion, there is growing interest in developing a personal spiritual life that is nourishing and that sustains gospel living and empowers us for mission.

CHARISM

Charism is a gift, generally a gift of God for the building up of the church. Saint Paul in 1 Corinthians 13 describes the various gifts. These gifts are charisms, gifts of God given to individuals and to groups for the good of all. Paul reminds us that there are only three lasting gifts or charisms, namely, faith, hope, and love, and the greatest of these is love. In the very next chapter Paul urges us to seek after the gift of prophecy, which is the ability to build, console, and encourage the people of God in their homeward journey.

Each religious institute is the recipient and guardian of such a gift or charism. The founding members received the gift or charism in a particular way and had the task of articulating that charism for the time and place in which they found themselves. Generally, this involved a particular experience of God, community, and mission. The experience of God gave rise to a spirituality and spiritual tradition that grew in depth and clarity over time with each succeeding generation. The experience of community enabled the group to grow and attract new members to live it, and share the charism. The experience of mission is a participation in the mission of Jesus. God is love and in love sends forth *(missio)* Jesus to announce good news to the people.

Each institute's charism is God's dream for the unfolding of creative love here and now. In a particular time and place an individual or group intuits this dream and seeks to articulate it, live and share it. Others are drawn to this dream; they resonate with it as it connects with their own God story, and they form a community.

Charism is caught by individuals and groups like succeeding waves of the ocean making a tidal flow. In every age the founding story is retold, both in words and in deeds. As it is brought to new times and places, the succeeding generations of the institute discover something uniquely new about the charism. The founding members may have said a great deal about the charism in medieval Europe, but if the charism is to continue, it must be a gift to those living it and to the people of God here and now. As succeeding generations live the charism, they drink deeply from the founding stories. Having been formed by those stories, they live out the charism in their own lives, writing new stories that shed further light on the gift/charism.

In the process of living the charism into succeeding generations, there is a dynamic interplay between the original vision and the movement of the Spirit here and now. There is an interaction between the ideal and the real in the unfolding of the story. The vision is spiritual and very human, and the living of it will be both spiritual and human. As successive generations live the charism, they are challenged to explore the essential elements of the life and the nonessential elements. There are some merely historical practices that can be left aside. There are other practices that, while not essential, have proved to be helpful in sustaining the charism. Other values are essential, and without them, the life could not be what it is. For example, the truly essential core of religious life is following Christ. The three vows of poverty, chastity, and obedience have proved themselves valuable in framing the life of consecration in following Christ. Over the history of religious life, there have been other ways of framing the life; for example, hermits fled to the desert, Benedictines have a different formulation of the vows, and some societies of apostolic life do not profess vows at all. There have been other particular forms that are merely historical, valuable in their own time and place but not translating well into other times and places. For example, at one time sisters wore widow's garb to enable them to move freely about the city to do ministry. This became the characteristic long black habit and veil of many religious communities, which took on a different significance over time. More recently, communities have reevaluated the origin of this practice and modified it in keeping with today's society.

Charism as gift comes into play at many levels. Religious life itself is a charism, a gift of more singular lifelong focus on spirituality, community, and ministry. There are many forms of religious life—monastic, evangelical, apostolic, and more. Each of these is another charism that shapes the charism of religious life. More specifically, religious orders and congregations are a particular expression of these charisms and a further charism themselves as they live a particular experience of God, community, and mission. We may even speak of individuals and groups within a congregation having a particular charism, a particular expression of their institute's charism. This may be a particular ministry or a vision for renewing their community or founding a new community. This can be done within the community, or it may involve moving away from their current community to live with integrity their particular charism. It frequently happens within the history of religious life that individuals or groups from one institute move out of their congregation to form a new community. The new group may bring the same charism to another geographic region or to another place in the life of the church or society. Separate groups may also be founded due to ideological differences, sometimes involving acrimonious disputes among varying factions. In the past, disputants occasionally resorted to violence and imprisonment against one another. But over time, both the original group and the new group may flourish, all doing honor to the original founding story. Religious life is a gift of the Spirit, and there seems to flow from this Spirit an unlimited variety of expressions of religious life.

Eastern Christianity also has a broad experience with religious life, and its experience of charism is distinct from that of the Christian West. In the East, religious life is seen as a movement rooted in apostolic times and flowing through various times and places with distinctive features. The desert hermits, the village ascetics, the wandering seeker featured in *The Way of a Pilgrim,* and the monks of Mount Athos are all part of a movement that is larger than any one of them. Their rule of life is the gospel, which is adapted to the time, place, and circumstances of each local community. The East has not had the West's experience of a divergence of orders and congregations. Instead, all religious men and women are part of this movement which has been present in diverse times and places from the earliest apostolic times right down to our present age, in a certain apostolic succession, analogous to that of the bishops. In the East, from the Council of Constantinople, the foundation of a new community required the permission of the bishop; that permission was simply a permission to found a community, not an approbation of the community's way of life. In Western Christianity, by contrast, approval of communities by bishops came much later, and it had a much more juridical tone. Approval was given to a written description of the life the community proposed to live, namely, its rule or constitution. Thus, bishops were more deeply involved in the shaping of new foundations by their ability to give or withhold this approval.

Another distinctive feature of Eastern religious life is its relationship to the bishops. While the East has always had married priests, bishops are required to be celibate. This gave rise to the practice of drawing bishops from monasteries, where celibacy was the normal practice. Thus many of the bishops were religious, and they had a deeper lived experience of religious life. This colored the relationship between religious communities and bishops. The East still considers religious life a distinctive state of life alongside priesthood and lay life. The West has become ambivalent on this issue. Vatican II proclaimed that religious life was not a distinctive state of life but that it draws from the lay state and the clerical state (*Lumen Gentium,* nos.

31, 43–44). However, over the decades since the council, church documents have often used the traditional formulation of three states: lay, religious, and clerical (*Vita Consecrata*, nos. 4, 30, 60). With the renewed ecclesiology of the council, it is generally understood that religious life holds a distinctive place within the broader Christian community, though some would question the ongoing significance of the life.

Religious life evolved in Eastern Christianity as a unified movement with diverse expressions and local communities participating in the movement. Religious life evolved in Western Christianity as an ever-widening diversity of institutes, congregations, and orders. As each seeks to claim its identity, it sometimes becomes difficult to figure out exactly how many different ways there are of living the same gospel, following the same Christ. Now, in the twenty-first century, the collaboration among congregations and orders is much more extensive. Intercommunity programs and ministries are common. Those coming to religious life today participate in intercommunity vocation discernment programs and then in intercommunity formation programs, both locally among various charisms, and nationally among various institutes of the same charism. This is a real counterpoint to the congregational isolation of the twentieth century, in which separation from the laity and from other religious institutes was the norm. Large communities in the same geographic region often competed with one another for opportunities for service and for the young men and women who sought entrance to religious life in unprecedented numbers.

The growing inter-congregational activity takes place in ministries that are co-sponsored by several religious communities in order to share expertise and resources. Consider, for example, the various social service projects, educational projects, and justice projects that were designed and built from the ground up by sisters collaborating from several different congregations. In addition, there is an increasing number of religious from one congregation serving in the institutions founded by another congregation. Members entering religious life in the last several decades often have the opportunity to serve in these intercommunity projects. All of this is giving rise to a greater intercommunity consciousness, a sense that we are all part of a movement of religious life that is greater than any one of our congregations. As this grows and develops, it occurs to me that we are becoming more like the East, where religious are part of a movement and there is a natural organic collaboration among institutes.

The first seed of newness is charism, which we see coming together in mutually enriching ways. The differences and boundaries between and among the various religious institutes may be less important as their shared values become central. The discussion of charism has led us naturally to begin talking about community, our next seed of newness.

COMMUNITY

Up to the present day, intercommunity activity has been most prominent in ministries and in formation. There are many sisters who have had opportunities to live in communities with religious from other congregations. They generally report that this is a very enriching experience because the group shares so much in common with members of the various religious institutes. However, today we also witness a decreasing number of women in many local community houses. Often sisters live in houses of one, two, or three, where they have lived for decades in the same configuration. As members move away or retire, there are fewer active members. However, these houses remain open so that the sisters can maintain their presence in a local area and remain close to the ministries they serve.

Many of the women who have been in religious life fifty years or more state that religious life is all about mission. This has been their experience, and they have done amazing works in support of the people among whom they live. However, those who have entered religious life in the last few decades challenge this thinking. Today, men and women are able to do mission in a variety of ways without entering religious life. In fact, those who choose to enter religious life generally have to take several years away from mission in order to fulfill the requirements of their institute's formation program. These new members say that they could have done ministry anywhere, sometimes with more freedom than their counterparts in religious communities. They could have obtained their education and developed a true professional competence in education, healthcare, theology, pastoral ministry, and other areas. Many people are doing this today and building up the ministries of the church.

Those coming to religious life in the twenty-first century are coming for community. They acknowledge the centrality of ministry and spirituality in their lives, but the unique difference they seek in religious life is community, and the particular form of community that is framed by vowed life. The new communities they seek are communities of praxis, communities that are dedicated first to living the gospel personally and interpersonally. They commit to supporting one another in lives of prayer, contemplation, and personal growth. They seek to live simply, justly, and sustainably making the day-to-day choices that this commitment demands. These communities of deliberate gospel living are centers of witness to authentic Christianity and also centers from which members can go out in service just as so many generations of religious have done before them. Likely they will not be armies of workers, but they will seek to live and serve in a world thirsting for deep spiritual values. As we explore the notion of community in religious life today, we look first at the elements of community that are emerging.

Elements of Community

Communities are local in character. Members of large national or international communities have been blessed by their connections with members in diverse geographic regions. However, as the numbers become fewer, there is a tension between maintaining a presence of one or two in different local areas and the desire to maintain connections with the larger group. This reality has led some to seek intercommunity relationships with members of other religious institutes. This allows them to remain in a local area but still to be nourished by the company of sisters who can support one another in prayer, life, and ministry. Religious are beginning to explore the possibilities of intercommunity housing so that they can build vibrant communities for mission. As they come into these communities, they will come with their history and experience as sisters from various traditions. However, as they begin to build communities together, something distinct will emerge. They will not be better than their various communities of origin. Instead, they will be today's communities, better adapted to today's reality.

Communities are relational. One of the insights of contemporary intentional communities is the importance of the relationships they form. Far from being an autonomous, self-sufficient group, the local community learns to balance internal coherence with external relationships. Relationships with neighbors, other faith-based groups, and other intentional communities in the area are critical to sustaining a community through its rocky founding years and through the challenges that inevitably come as the group grows and becomes established. These relationships are mutual, so that while friends, neighbors, and colleagues can help the local religious community, the community can offer its growing resources and experience to assist others. In addition to relationship with other local groups, the communities of religious can network among themselves regionally, nationally, and internationally.

Twenty-First-Century Leadership

In the past, relationships were largely provided by membership in the same congregation. When they were founded, the governance structures of these communities mirrored the governance structures of church and state in medieval Europe. Even more recent foundations often kept the hierarchical structures inherited from that era. The Second Vatican Council spoke to governance within the church. One of its key insights was the importance of subsidiarity; the council taught that decisions and authority in the church should not be concentrated at the top of the chain of hierarchy. Instead, decisions should be made at the lowest level, closest to the people affected by the decision. The notion of subsidiarity came out of a hierarchical system, and it is based on the assumption that the power resides at the top, but that it should be pushed to the lowest possible level. Federation as a governance concept is the mirror image of subsidiarity, though it may look the same from the outside. In a federation the assumption is that the power lies at the bottom, with the individuals and groups. When the individuals and groups come into relationship, they retain their own power and authority. However, they yield to a central authority those responsibilities that are best handled centrally. The United States was originally organized as a federation, under the Articles of Confederation, but soon the country reorganized under the Constitution, with more central power. Less than one hundred years later, the southern states seceded to form a confederacy, returning power to the states. The proper balance of local, state, and federal power continues to be debated.

In the communities that are evolving, the notion of federation may be more useful than the hierarchy-subsidiarity duo that has been at work in the church and in religious life for much of its recent history. Under this model, communities would form locally and regain a large degree of local autonomy. Decisions about prayer, community, ministry, housing, and finance would all be handled at the local level by those living in the community, the people who will be affected by the decisions. They are in the best position to make and implement choices. They can then network with other local communities in relationships of mutual benefit. It makes sense to have some pooling of resources, financial cooperation, and collaboration in welcoming and incorporating new members. (This is discussed in more detail in Chapter 5.)

It is in community that we find salvation from the various forms of fragmentation that plague our society. Even more, it is in community that we meet the other in a place of mutual respect and reciprocal support and challenge as we move forward on our journey. In small intentional communities we meet Christ and are challenged to live the gospel and the values we profess. We build up, encourage, and challenge one another as we journey together in personal development and spiritual growth as well as in our work for sustainability and justice. Small local communities do not have power or prestige, and so they cannot be easily coopted by systems of power. They do not have to play it safe, to protect investments, preserve resources, or placate powerful interests.

The smallness of the communities gives them an agility that allows them to commit to values, unhampered by institutional ties that restrain the larger, more settled religious institutes of today. The larger religious communities have found ways to use their corporate power for mission and for making a difference in the halls of power. The smaller emerging communities will not have this power; instead, their power is in the strength of their witness and the loftiness of their ideals. Smaller groups will not need highly structured processes of discernment, consultation, and decision making. Decisions will not be made in conference rooms but in living rooms. The groups will have the agility to respond to issues of pressing importance of the day. The actions they take can be decided over dinner—and they can carry them into action the next morning. They will have to live with the consequences, with no one but themselves to blame for failure. This is the price they will pay for the freedom to live deliberately and act swiftly and decisively in response to the Spirit's call. Like Catholic Workers and other Christian anarchists, they can repudiate systems of power, yet claim the personal power that they hold. This power, humbly acknowledged, can be placed at the service of the Spirit, in community and in mission.

As we progress deeper into the twenty-first century, we find ourselves in the midst of a postmodern world, and we are learning more about leadership in this new cultural context. Postmoderns are characterized by smaller groups that network for mutual benefit. Shunning all vestiges of hierarchy, they seek to empower individuals to work creatively for the benefit of all.

One of the images of leadership that can be helpful is developed by Ori Brafman and Rod Beckstrom in *The Starfish and the Spider*.[6] They explore some aspects of leadership in a postmodern world, contrasting the spider, with its centralized body systems, and the starfish, whose body systems are decentralized. The spider has a head and a central nervous system. Its digestive system is efficient and processes nourishment for its whole body. Its movement system, coordinated by the nervous system, is highly developed and allows for complex movement, the spinning of webs. Through chemical signals it coordinates with other spiders in a colony. The starfish has its body systems organized in a circular network. Each arm of the starfish has all the components needed for life, and the five arms share resources through a neural network and a circular digestive tract. This arrangement allows the starfish to function even if one or more of its arms is injured. It has no head or central control, so each of its arms can continue to function even if others are compromised. Brafman and Beckstrom propose this as a model of "leader-less" organization. These organizations empower individuals to use their own authority and to take responsibility for their own lives and their own path. Like arms of the starfish, people have what they need to survive and thrive; coordination with peers can bring benefit to the whole organization.

Religious life at its best calls members to move beyond personal autonomy and into community. It provides a forum for members to take responsibility for their own lives and to take responsibility for one another as well, in a spirit of interdependence. Many religious communities have transitioned out of the highly centralized and very hierarchical leadership structures of

---

[6] Ori Brafman and Rod A. Beckstrom, *The Starfish and the Spider: The Unstoppable Power of Leaderless Organizations* (New York: Portfolio Trade, 2008).

the nineteenth and twentieth centuries. These structures enabled the building and coordination of large institutional ministries in education and healthcare. However, as we move deeper into the twenty-first century, these ministries are gradually being transferred to very competent lay leadership or being replaced by other service organizations or by governmental agencies. The smaller local communities will focus their energies on other unmet needs in their local area, sometimes working in small groups, other times working in ministries organized and directed by others. They will not have the resources to continue to maintain the elaborate healthcare and educational institutions of the nineteenth and twentieth centuries, but they do not need the extensive leadership structures called for by those institutional networks.

There are examples of this type of organization in the history of religious life. In many monastic traditions small local communities were the norm. Some of these communities were purposely limited to six or twelve members, both to limit groups to a manageable size in terms of space and support as well as to avoid potential problems linked with amassing wealth and power. Other monasteries were allowed to grow into virtual cities, remaining independent of control by other monasteries or by the bishops. Centralization of orders began with the Franciscans and Dominicans, who sought to combat the extravagant wealth of some medieval monasteries. This centralization was common in apostolic orders as well, but there were exceptions. The Sisters of St. Joseph were founded in the south of France in 1650. Their original organizational structure was decentralized, with small local communities organized throughout the region. This organizational structure proved beneficial during the French Revolution, because there was no central structure to suppress. Local houses could be disbanded, but houses in remote villages could continue to operate if the local population was sympathetic to their cause. After the French Revolution the community was reorganized. Under the leadership of Mother St. John Fontbonne, the community became much more highly centralized. This enabled it to spread rapidly in the early nineteenth century and to send sisters to remote regions, including the frontiers of the United States. Communities founded in the United States soon severed ties with the French congregation in order to have more autonomy and to be able to respond more efficiently and rapidly to the growing needs in this country. These congregations utilized both centralized and decentralized leadership, with their benefits and challenges.

Today's religious life will likely benefit from the leadership studies and cultural thinkers who propose decentralized, leader-less structures of self-organized local communities that are networked in meaningful ways. While some organizations proliferate through local units or cells, we are coming into an era where we see prophetic cells springing up in the form of intentional communities whose lives speak a word of truth and encouragement to those seeking light in these challenging times.

We have explored seeds of newness in charism. Charisms evolved with greater and greater specificity. They are now beginning to merge as communities discover that what unites them is greater than what divides them, and that shared ministries, projects, and communities are bringing new life to their congregations. Charisms are a particular way of articulating a vision for living the gospel. As these charisms are lived into succeeding centuries, they respond to particular changing circumstances while maintaining fidelity to their founding inspiration. As we move forward, communities are finding more and more in common. They are coming to a consciousness of a common story of religious life, through the centuries, across the globe, and even across the lines of various religious families. This may evolve in some places into a new understanding of religious life as a movement whose local communities are autonomous but related to the wider whole.

CONNECTIVITY

Our world is more connected than it has ever been in the past. The phrase "global village" was coined in the 1960s by Marshall

McLuhan to describe the effect of the expanding mass media on society.[7] At that time radio and television were expanding their influence and building larger and larger audiences. The term is used to describe how cities and towns, states and regions, and whole countries are contracted into a village by means of the new electronically mediated forms of communication. Whereas in the past information might take weeks or months to move across the country, these media brought an unprecedented immediacy to news and information. In the 1960s they brought images of the Kennedy assassination, the moon landings, and the Vietnam war to the living rooms of most American homes. According to McLuhan, this change in communication media actually changes human awareness and our sense of responsibility for global events.

McLuhan further predicted that ongoing developments in communication media would continue to affect human consciousness and the ways in which social movements developed. The Internet has provided this ongoing development of communication, and the shift in social consciousness is being felt increasingly as politics, business, education, and church all find themselves scrambling to get up to speed with the new media and find ways of using them to benefit their causes. The Internet allows individuals and groups to establish a public presence at very little cost. With an Internet presence everyone has instant access to the quarter of a billion US Internet users as well as to the two-and-a-quarter billion Internet users worldwide.[8] These users constitute one-third of the world's population. Google, one of the top web indexing services, reported in 2008 that it was already indexing over one trillion websites.[9] That number has continued to grow at increasing rates. That means that

---

[7] Marshall McLuhan, *The Gutenberg Galaxy: The Making of Typographic Man* (Toronto: University of Toronto Press, 1962); Marshall McLuhan, *Understanding Media: The Extensions of Man* (New York: McGraw-Hill, 1964).

[8] Miniwatts Marketing Group, "Internet World Stats," n.d., internetworldstats.com website.

[9] Google, "We Knew the Web Was Big," Google Official Blog, n.d., googleblog.blogspot.com website.

there are nearly five hundred websites for every Internet user in the world. Cyberspace is awash in information, images, video, and sounds, and there are throngs of Internet users searching through the endless stream of data for information that is useful, informative, or inspiring.

Social media burst onto the already prolific World Wide Web in the 1990s and added yet another dimension to these media. Social media use the infrastructure already available on the Internet to facilitate relationships among individuals and groups. Mark Zuckerberg, president and founder of Facebook, was studying computer science and psychology at Harvard when he asked himself how the tools of computer science could be put at the service of human relationships. The result led to the launch of the first version of Facebook in 2004. Less than ten years later, in 2012, Facebook topped one billion users, or one out of every seven men, women, and children on the planet. Facebook users are more numerous than the population of every country except India and China, and it may soon surpass even them.

The ongoing evolution of the means of social communication is affecting all aspects of society. It is changing the way business is done, the way political campaigns are run, and even the way the gospel is preached. One striking example of the way new media changes the landscape of society is the Arab Spring. In spring of 2011, Wael Gohnim used Facebook and Twitter to catalyze a popular uprising in Egypt. He did not create the unrest, but his communication brought together likeminded Egyptians and effectively challenged the presidency of Hosni Mubarak. In this, Gohnim is much like Thomas Paine, the pamphleteer of the American Revolution, whose *Common Sense* catalyzed and sustained the colonists. Gohnim used popular media to galvanize the resistance and unite disparate parties into an effective force on the political landscape. The web of relationships formed by social media provides the forum for groups to organize and move into action.

The ongoing evolution of the means of social communication is also affecting religious life, particularly the lives of younger and middle-aged religious. Women and men in this cohort connect naturally via social media and instinctively form meaningful relationships with their peers across the country from various congregations. They may have only a few peers in their own congregation, but the online world opens many possibilities for building supportive relationships. These webs of relationship are changing the way religious relate among themselves.

Connectivity affects how communities are built, organized, and sustained, and it affects the way charisms are lived. Social media forums are allowing religious to connect across the country and around the world with others in their own congregation and other congregations. These forums provide for the mutual support of members who may be one of just a few in their age cohort within their own congregation. In addition, these conversations turn to the future of religious life, asking questions about what religious life will look like in the next ten, twenty, or thirty years as the dominant cohort passes on. Certainly congregations will be smaller, and median ages will continue to rise. However, even as this happens, the minority cohorts will remain the minority for at least another twenty years, if the current vocation rates remain steady.

These conversations are sources of support and circles of visioning. Those who engage in these conversations are sharing insights about the future of religious life as seen from their eyes. Often they share these insights with their own communities, providing fresh insights and an alternate voice. However, in the self-organized peer circles, their experience and insights are shared, affirmed, and echoed back. They can grow and develop as women with forty, sixty, or even eighty years of religious life ahead of them and share the vision of what will be. These women are developing a voice that is distinct but complementary to the voices of women with forty, sixty, or even eighty years of religious life behind them.

Connectivity gives rise to forums, and these forums are empowering younger religious to find and share their voice. A distinctive voice is arising as post–Vatican II, twenty-first-century women are naming a new truth. These forums were the seed bed in which many of the insights in this book were first voiced, challenged, and refined. I take full responsibility for what I write; it is not a report on the conversations I have had. However, I would be remiss if I did not acknowledge the gift that these circles are as together we discuss the experience, perspective, and insights we bring. There is an ongoing cycle of reflection and contemplation, whose fruits are shared in rich conversation, which is brought back to reflection and contemplation, and so on. This is giving rise to a distinctive voice that speaks from a new consciousness of the movement of the Spirit within and among us and a newness emerging in religious life.

CONSCIOUSNESS

A new consciousness is arising among us: evolutionary consciousness, postmodernism, or simply a new consciousness. It is a new sense of being in the world, a new sense of our place in the universe.

> The dynamic world of evolution with its interplay of chance and law is a very different world. . . . The concept of being within an evolutionary context has changed. . . . Every being exists in a web of relationships that both gives rise to the entity and shapes its character.[10]

One of the starting places of the new consciousness is the first view of the earth from space in 1968. British cosmologist Sir Fred Hoyle, in 1948, was prescient in his prediction that the first images of earth from space would have a deep and lasting effect on our view of our own planet.[11] All our lives, all our family and friends, all our hopes and dreams, the lives of our most ancient ancestors and our children's children are found on this planet. Most of the ancients knew only their own village and the few

---

[10] Ilia Delio, *Christ in Evolution* (Maryknoll, NY: Orbis Books, 2008), 32.

[11] Steve Connor, "Forty Years Since the First Picture of Earth from Space," *The Independent* (London), January 10, 2009, independent.co.uk website.

surrounding villages. Then, with the growth of transportation and communication, great empires were built, and the human family woke up to a wider and wider sense of peoples, tribes, and nations. This came to be painfully present as two world wars involved great portions of the human family in bloody conflict. But from that conflict the human family came to a new consciousness of itself with the establishment of the United Nations in 1945 and the proclamation of the Universal Declaration on Human Rights in 1948. In the 1960s, for the first time, this planet was seen not as the vast, varied, and populous place that the human family had come to know, but as a tiny blue marble hanging delicately in space, surrounded by a deep darkness against a starry curtain composed of our cosmic neighbors. This image is commonplace in our age, and children take for granted the brilliant images in their science textbooks, images that startled their grandparents less than fifty years earlier. As Hoyle had predicted, this has forever changed the self-consciousness of the human family and given us a new understanding of our place in the universe and our reality as a global family.

A second element of the new consciousness is the pace of change. It has become commonplace to refer to the increasing pace of change, and this acceleration has been quantified. First formulated in 1965, Moore's law states that the power of computers doubles every two years.[12] This law has been applied to more and more sectors of technology from semiconductors to nanotechnology to the increasing use of computers in education, in business, and in personal use. Social media is expanding exponentially, connecting more and more people across the globe. This not only changes the media we use to communicate, but it speeds up the pace of communication and increases the potential audience of a message.

An analysis of the history of technology shows that technological change is exponential, contrary to the common-sense "intuitive linear" view. So we won't experience one hundred

---

[12] Gordon E. Moore, "Cramming More Components onto Integrated Circuits," *Electronics Magazine* 38, no. 8 (April 19, 1965): 2–5.

years of progress in the twenty-first century—it will be more like twenty thousand years of progress (at today's rate). The "returns," such as chip speed and cost-effectiveness, also increase exponentially. There's even exponential growth in the rate of exponential growth. Within a few decades machine intelligence will surpass human intelligence, leading to the Singularity— technological change so rapid and profound it represents a rupture in the fabric of human history.[13]

All this change broadens the gap between generations. Marc Prensky coined the term "digital native" to refer to the children born in a world that was computerized and connected. This generation relates to the new technologies as natives, while their parents and teachers relate to the same technologies as immigrants. But even beyond their adept use of computers and other electronic gadgets, this generation thinks differently.[14] The next generation is likely to be even further removed as the pace of change continues to accelerate.

With the increasing rate of change there also comes increasing complexity. This has been identified at the biological level as living systems evolved from simple organic molecules to single-celled creatures to multi-cellular and multi-system animals and then to the complex neurological systems of the human brain. Humans are self-conscious and are able to build complex structures outside themselves and even to build "thinking machines." We come into relationship with one another and build societies that are greater than the sum of their parts. We connect with one another through thought and through relationships. In 1926, Russian geochemist Vladimir Vernadsky (1863–1945) coined the term *noosphere* to describe this stage of development.[15] The geosphere is the nonliving stuff of the

---

[13] Ray Kurzweil, *The Age of Spiritual Machines: When Computers Exceed Human Intelligence* (New York: Penguin Books, 2000), 32.

[14] Marc Prensky, "Digital Natives, Digital Immigrants," two parts, *On the Horizon 9*, no. 5 (October 2001), 1–6, and no. 6 (December 2001): 1–6.

[15] Vladimir Vernadsky, "The Biosphere and the Noosphere," *American Scientist 33*, no. 1 (1945): 1–12; idem, *The Biosphere: Complete Annotated Edition*, ed. M. A. S. McMenamin, trans. D. B. Langmuir (1926; New York: Springer, 1998).

universe, the galaxies, stars, and planets. On our planet the biosphere has developed, a layer of living things, plants, and animals that grows on the geosphere. The biosphere shapes the geosphere and is in turn sustained by it. Vernadsky then posited a noosphere, a sphere of human thought that grows on the biosphere. The noosphere shapes the biosphere and geosphere, and is in turned sustained by them. The World Wide Web and social media seem to be the incarnation of Vernadsky's ideas.

Pierre Teilhard de Chardin (1881–1955), a Jesuit paleontologist, saw the physical universe created by God and shot through with divine Presence. He understood the universe as continuously evolving in a process he called "cosmogenesis." This is in opposition to the notion of a static universe. The universe is unfolding, and in this unfolding there is ever-greater meaning; the trajectory of evolution is toward complexity and consciousness. Inert elements, atoms, and molecules came together to form the first living cells. This happened through the interplay of randomness, the laws of nature, and the inner imperative of creation. Inert matter seems to be "groping" *(tâtonnement)*, reaching beyond itself, to form a living being that is greater than the sum of its parts. Living beings also have this same evolutionary imperative reaching beyond themselves to sentient beings, then to being conscious of themselves. This consciousness allows humans to open to one another in relationship and to open to God and to respond to God who is Love. Teilhard saw this movement as evidence of Christ living in the heart of the universe, specifically in the heart of the material universe, and bringing it back to God. Cosmogenesis is neither mere chance nor purely mechanistic. Creation also has within itself the inner imperative driving it relentlessly to Christ, whom Teilhard called the Omega point.[16] In the unfolding story of the evolving universe, we see God's "plan for the fullness of time, to gather up all things in him [Christ], things in heaven and things on earth" (Eph 1:10).

---

[16] Teilhard de Chardin, *The Future of Man* (New York: Image, 2004), 115, 178, 185, 205.

The changing consciousness affects all aspects of our lives. It affects the world in which religious life is situated. It affects the men and women who are choosing religious life today. It changes the way people think about life and the world. The notion of being is supplanted by the notion of becoming. Meta-narratives that formed the fundamental assumptions of the twentieth century are no longer even meaningful conversations. There is a preference for small, self-organizing groups. Networks replace hierarchies. Federation replaces subsidiarity. Our lives are defined by the decisions we make and the company we keep, rather than by mission statements and static doctrines. As it moves into the future, religious life will thrive to the extent that it is able to let go of the past and engage the future. Moving away from dualism, we engage a God who is completely here and now, embedded in the fabric of life, and who is at the same time completely Other. The early Christians, particularly in the East, were comfortable with the mystical and allegorical. Through the centuries that has shifted toward a more fact-based religion that moderns have embraced. Postmoderns are finding more resonance with the early Christian sensibilities, returning to an orientation to the mystical, but one deeply immersed in a modern scientific world view.

CONTEMPLATION

The final seed of newness that we should examine is that of contemplation. This is certainly related to the new consciousness, but it speaks more directly to the spiritual orientation of the day. Karl Rahner wrote that "the Christian of the future will be a mystic or will not exist at all." He explains that mysticism is "a genuine experience of God emerging from the very heart of our existence."[17] Franciscan theologian Ilia Delio sees this move to the mystical as "essential to developing theology in the second axial period of the third millennium."[18]

---

[17] Karl Rahner, *Theological Investigations,* vol. 20, *Concern for the Church* (New York: Crossroad, 1981), 149ff.

[18] Ilia Delio, *Christ in Evolution* (Maryknoll, NY: Orbis Books, 2008), 68.

Mysticism and contemplation have been an important element of the Christian experience from the earliest Christian centuries. New Testament writers speak of the deep personal experience of God. Paul writes: "It is no longer I who live, but it is Christ who lives in me. And the life I now live in the flesh I live by faith in the Son of God, who loved me and gave himself for me" (Gal 2:20). John writes: "God is love, and those who abide in love abide in God, and God abides in them" (1 Jn 4:16; see also Eph 4:6, 2 Cor 12:2–6). Christian writers in the second and third centuries picked up this theme describing the dynamic of the incarnation as a process of kenosis, God becoming human, for the purpose of theosis, humans becoming God. Irenaeus of Lyon (130–200) wrote: "Our Lord Jesus Christ, who did, through His transcendent love, become what we are, that He might bring us to be even what He is Himself."[19] This kenosis-theosis dynamic was an important part of Eastern Christian spirituality from the early centuries and continues to be a living part of the theology and spirituality of the Eastern Christian Churches today. The same kenosis-theosis dynamic inspired countless men and women to flee to the desert to take up a more intense spiritual life.

This same longing for God inspired the monastic movements, both East and West. Dionysius and Evagrius articulated the classical understanding of the mystical path as a threefold journey of the purgative, illuminative, and unitive ways.[20] The purgative way invites the Christian to live the gospel, to do good and not do evil. The illuminative way invites the good person to develop a spiritual life, devoting time to prayer and reading of the scriptures and spiritual writers. The unitive way opens for the spiritual person who enters into a deeper union with the Divine. Later spiritual writers affirmed this

---

[19] Philip Schaff, Alexander Roberts, and James Donaldson, eds., *The Early Church Fathers—Ante-Nicene Fathers*, vol. 1, *The Apostolic Fathers: Justin Martyr and Irenaeus* (New York: Charles Scribner, 1913), Book 5, "Preface."

[20] See John Anthony McGuckin, *The Book of Mystical Chapters: Meditations on the Soul's Ascent, from the Desert Fathers and Other Early Christian Contemplatives* (Boston: Shambhala, 2003).

basic insight and stressed the fact that these three ways are integrated in every Christian who seeks to live a serious spiritual life. Each of us will struggle at times with doing the right thing (purgative), with a commitment to prayer (illuminative), and with accepting God's invitation to an intimate personal relationship (unitive).

Later writers added two more important insights to the understanding of the basic spiritual path. The first of these is the experience described as the dark night by the sixteenth-century Spanish mystic Saint John of the Cross (1542–91).[21] The phrase refers to a felt sense of the absence of God. It is not a true absence but the feeling of the absence of God, who is the complete fulfillment of the human spirit. This felt absence causes the person to seek the God of love ever more urgently, yet without ever finding the merest hint of the Divine. The very experience of seeking expands the human spirit and refines the intuition for the full presence of God. But the person cannot understand the purpose and generous gift of this period until he or she is once again able to experience the full felt presence of God. Evelyn Underhill describes it as "the gateway to a higher state."[22] Frank Viola uses the image of God walking off the stage, leaving the person profoundly alone.[23]

Another insight into the contemplative life is the understanding that it is intimately related to the active life. The person is deeply united with God in a way that is both active and passive:

> It remains a paradox of the mystics that the passivity at which they appear to aim is really the most intense activity: more, that where it is wholly absent no great creative action can take place. In it, the superficial self compels itself to be still, in order that it may liberate another more

---

[21] John of the Cross, *John of the Cross: Selected Writings*, ed. Kieran Kavanaugh (New York: Paulist Press, 1988), 155ff.

[22] Evelyn Underhill, *Mysticism* (1911; Digireads.com, 2005), 258.

[23] Frank Viola, *Revise Us Again: Living from a Renewed Christian Script* (New York: David C. Cook, 2011), 80.

deep-seated power that is, in the ecstasy of the contemplative genius, raised to the highest pitch of efficiency.[24]

William James (1842–1910) in his classic work *The Varieties
of Religious Experience* named four characteristics of mystical
experience: (1) ineffability; (2) noetic or integrated quality; (3)
transiency; and (4) passivity.[25] From this divine union, the person goes forth in apostolic action which comes from the place
of deep union.

John of Ruysbroeck (1293–1381) writes:

> He is just and truthful in all things, and he possesses a
> rich and a generous ground, which is set in the richness
> of God: and therefore he must always spend himself on
> those who have need of him; for the living fount of the
> Holy Ghost, which is his wealth, can never be spent. And
> he is a living and willing instrument of God, with which
> God works whatsoever He wills and howsoever He wills
> and these works he reckons not as his own, but gives all
> the glory to God.[26]

This mystical way underwent its own "dark night" beginning
in the centuries of the Reformation and Counter-Reformation,
when both Catholics and Protestants were very sensitive to
the divisions between them and very concerned to ensure that
people remained loyal to their religious affiliation. One aspect
of this was careful attention to the words used to express the
prayers and beliefs of Christians. Catechisms abounded, and
theologians turned to the work of distinguishing orthodox
belief and practices from the heresies that were propounded by

---

[24] Underhill, *Mysticism*, 40.

[25] William James, *The Varieties of Religious Experience* (Cambridge, MA:
Harvard University Press, 1985), 380.

[26] John of Ruysbroeck, "Sparkling Stone," in *The Adornment of the Spiritual
Marriage*, ed. Evelyn Underhill, trans. C. A. Wynschenk (London: J. M. Dent
and Sons, 1916). Chap. XIII.

their counterparts in other Christian denominations. Mysticism fell under suspicion because of its emphasis on personal experience and nameless encounter with the wholly other in sacred Mystery.

This trend is beginning to reverse itself as we move into the twenty-first century. There are many reasons for this change. Certainly the works of many contemporary theologians and spiritual writers have helped to bring this about. The widespread availability of classic spiritual writings and modern works is also helping to supply a need. But that need probably arises out of the change in consciousness described above. There is an openness to the sacred, and people are willing and able to find the resources and guides that feed their own personal spiritual growth. Thomas Merton (1915–68) was one of the most important spiritual writers of the twentieth century, and his popular books about his own spiritual journey and about the spiritual life helped to make contemplation accessible to the masses.

The late twentieth century also saw a renewal in spiritual practice. Ritual and liturgy that had sustained generations underwent renewal following the Second Vatican Council. People began to use a wider variety of spiritual practices that were aimed at cultivating a deeper spiritual life. These included age-old practices such as Lectio Divina, the Jesus Prayer, and icons. They explored physical elements of prayer, focusing on breathing, posture, and movement. Spiritual seekers came to benefit from spiritual direction and spiritual friendship, both of which are deeply rooted in the Christian mystical tradition. All of these practices provided seekers with a wealth of tools to assist in the growth of a deeper spiritual life.

The contemplative movement is an important part of contemporary religious experience. It is also an important seed of newness as we explore the emerging future of religious life. Over the centuries religious life has flourished when the Christian community flourishes, and particularly when there is a vibrant spiritual life flourishing within the Christian community. Many men and women who come to religious life today have already begun to take the spiritual life seriously. They come to grow and deepen that life and to find a community where that life is supported and nourished.

Rahner, as we have noted, said that the Christian of the future will be a mystic or will not exist at all. We might extend that to say that religious communities of the future will be communities of mystics or will not exist at all. This is the central role of these communities: to nourish and sustain a deep contemplative life among their members and to be centers of spirituality that can nourish and sustain that deep contemplative life in the wider Christian community.

CONCLUSION

We can identify many seeds of newness in contemporary society and particularly in emerging religious life. This chapter has sought to explore some of the key elements, though there are certainly others that could have been discussed. Attention to charism will be important as we explore the future, which may see a convergence of all the riches of these particular gifts. Community will take on a much greater importance for our church and world and is a primary reason why people are seeking out religious life today. Connectivity and the new consciousness allow us to organize in smaller local communities that are networked across the country and around the globe. And finally, the contemplative life is both a reason for coming to religious life and an important service that religious life can provide to the wider church and to society, which longs for a deeper and more meaningful spiritual life.

CHAPTER FOUR

REIMAGINING RELIGIOUS LIFE

In this chapter we turn to the task of reimagining religious life. In this task we reach instinctively for the tools of group discernment rather than those of strategic planning. We will gather in living rooms rather than conference rooms; we will use Skype and social media rather than study groups and five-year plans.

The first task is to reimagine the vows as life-enhancing covenants that seek to incarnate the beatitudes here and now. The vow of poverty invites us to create an alternate economy of simplicity of life and interdependence in community and in solidarity with the poor and marginalized. We can move to an economy of cooperation and mutual support rather than an economy of competition. It is not an option, but a necessity, if we are to form communities where we are radically committed to living the beatitudes. We reimagine the vow of celibate chastity as a freedom for relationship, in spirituality, in community, and in ministry. Our primary life commitment within the community frees us to live reconciling love in a particular way. Our vow of obedience enables us to create an alternate political system, one based not on power but on love and service. We are called to listen to one another and to build a humane lifestyle that resists the frenetic will to action and will to power. We acknowledge that we are not the saviors of the world but that our prophetic witness to gospel living is our greatest contribution to the in-breaking of the community of the beatitudes in our world. It is important that we make these commitments for life because this lifetime commitment affects the quality of our being together. This does not exclude the possibility of other forms of commitment lived in complementarity to the permanent vowed commitment.

We reimagine community as a privileged place where we can take seriously a commitment of living the gospel, deliberately integrating its values into the life of the community. We commit to living simply and sustainably and living lightly on the earth. We share our goods and live in reconciliation. We will choose to locate our communities in areas neglected by power brokers of this earth; these may be economically depressed areas or rural areas. From these places we will commit to deconstructing systematically the "-isms" that hold us and others in subjugation: racism, sexism, consumerism, and so on. The quality of this community will affect our lives, our spirituality, and our ministry to those in need.

We reimagine mission. Many of our communities were founded in a time when only religious could commit themselves full time to a life of ministry. Family commitments and gender stereotypes prohibited people, particularly women, from taking on lives of ministry. However, today it is commonplace for men and women to commit to ministry and to a life of service, not only within church settings but in the wider nonprofit and social sectors. Thus we will have to reimagine the place of ministry in this new social and ecclesial context.

Community itself will be a part of the mission of emerging religious life. The commitment to faith-based intentional community affects not only those who live it but those who live around it and share in various ways in the life of the community. At the same time the community may make deliberate choices to take on some form of service that it carries out as a group. While members will continue to seek ministry outside the local community, to assist with the sustenance of the group, it may also be helpful to have some community project. This may be as simple as rehabbing the living space or creating a garden where they grow some of their own food. One hundred years ago communities ministered together, and families worked together in a family business or family farm. In today's society ministry takes members out of community just as work takes people away from the family home. We don't hearken unrealistically back to a bygone day of total community, where life and ministry were all done completely together. But might we allow ourselves to imagine choosing a project for the community that brings us together and builds community and solidarity? Might we imagine balancing ministry and commitments outside the community with those within?

As a local community we can discern collectively when and how we can free one or more members to work at the margins, serving those who cannot otherwise be helped. Mission will also support community by ensuring our solidarity with the working poor and being an expression of our commitment to justice, spirituality, and sustainability.

REIMAGINING VOWS—
CREATING AN ALTERNATE WORLD

The three vows of poverty, chastity, and obedience have come to be synonymous with religious life. The vows have not always been formulated in the same way, and they are not the same for all religious communities. Even those religious institutes that profess the same three vows may have very distinct ways of understanding them and may have a unique way of formulating them and describing how they relate to their spirituality, community, and mission.

In the early Christian centuries religious dedicated themselves to a way of life and made particular commitments to prayer, to simplicity, and to solitude, and for the most part, these early religious were celibate. It was not till they gathered in communities that obedience to the community leader became the norm. Benedict required that his monks profess stability, that is, remaining in the monastery for life, obedience to the abbot, and fidelity to the monastic way of life (*conversatio mores*). Eastern monasteries did not begin the practice of profession of vows until much later. Instead, a person became a monk or nun by taking up religious dress and making a commitment to the direction of a spiritual guide. Even when the vows came to more widespread use in the East, they maintained the notion that one became a monk or a nun by living the life; profession of vows was merely an external manifestation of an internal reality. In the West, on the other hand, profession of the vows was both a spiritual offering and a juridical act by which a person became a member of the community.

Historically, the use of the traditional formulation of the three vows of poverty, chastity, and obedience began with the Franciscans and Dominicans of the twelfth and thirteenth centuries. Religious life needed more mobility to allow members to address the needs of the church and society. Communities were also becoming more centralized, in contrast to the autonomous Benedictine monasteries, in which stability was an important part of the life. At that time the vows of poverty, chastity, and obedience replaced stability and the monastic way of life as a way of giving form to the commitment to the religious life. They were seen as bonds that connected the individual members to the order and also as a way of offering a person's whole life to God in a way analogous to vowing stability in a monastery for life.

Over time the vows also took on various meanings. Vows were seen as a sacrifice of legitimate human goods of property, sexuality, and autonomy. Whether in its monastic form or the later mendicant form, religious life was called a white martyrdom; like the offering of the early Christian martyrs, religious gave their entire lives to God.[1] Vows were also seen as a means of union with God as described by John Paul II, citing Thomas Aquinas:

The purpose of religious vows is to scale the heights of love, a complete love, dedicated to Christ under the im-

---

[1] Philip Schaff, ed., *A Select Library of the Nicene and Post-Nicene Fathers of the Christian Church*, vol. 6, *Nicene and Post-Nicene Fathers II* (Edinburgh: T and T Clark, 1886), 299; Charles Plummer, *Vitae Sanctorum Hiberniae Partim Hactenus Ineditae Ad Fidem Codicum Manuscriptorum Recognovit Prolegomenis Notis Indicibus Instruxit*, vol. 1 (Oxford: Clarendon Press, 1910), cxix, note 7.

pulse of the Holy Spirit and, through Christ, offered to the Father. Hence there is the value of the obligation and consecration of religious profession which in the Eastern and Western Christian tradition is considered as a *baptismus flaminis* (baptism of the Spirit), inasmuch as "a person's heart is moved by the Holy Spirit to believe in and love God, and to repent of sin."[2]

The vows have also been interpreted as practical means of organizing community with an orientation to mission. By celibacy, members are freed from family attachments; by poverty, they renounce personal gain and free resources for mission; and by obedience, the members are formed into a ready labor force and sent to where they are most needed, without reference to personal preferences.

It is probably true that for many religious communities and for many veteran religious, the meaning and purpose of the vows have changed over time. While they remain steadfast in their commitment, the vows shape the life that they live. At a certain point they are no longer constraints but simply a way of life, freely chosen, and a blessing to professed religious who acknowledge the vows as simultaneously gift, sacrifice, and pathway.

The vows contain juridical elements that tell the religious what is and is not permissible. Celibacy prohibits marriage, poverty prohibits independent use of goods, obedience requires conformity with constitutions and legitimate commands (*Code of Canon Law*, canons 600–602). They also contain spiritual elements, often in the same sentence of canon law or in the same article of the constitutions or rule. The vow of celibacy prohibits marriage as it invites the religious to be "unavailable" for exclusive or sexual relationships, making him or her more available to form healthy adult relationships in community and in ministry.

---

[2] John Paul II, "Consecrated Life Is Rooted in Baptism," General Audience, Rome, October 26, 1994, citing Thomas Aquinas, *Summa Theol.*, III, q. 66, a. 11.

The vow of poverty is not only about what religious possess, but also about how they possess it, their interior attitudes toward those possessions and living in interdependence. Obedience is not only about adhering to community constitutions and rules, but also about learning to listen deeply for the voice and word of God in all things and responding ever more fully and freely.

In this section I turn to another interpretation of the vows. It is not intended to supplant other theologies of vowed life. Instead, it is a reimagining that may offer new vitality to the age-old practices of vowed life in community with a particular attention to the prophetic aspects of the vows. In this section I rely on Sandra Schneiders's work on this topic.[3]

Poverty as Alternate Economy

The vow of poverty has been lived by thousands of committed religious over the course of the centuries. Following the invitation of Jesus, they have gone, sold, given, and followed (Mk 10:21). They have believed in the importance to the spiritual quest of divestment, of simplicity, and of sharing. They have taken seriously the economy of the beatitudes: blessed are the poor, the merciful, the meek, for theirs is the kingdom of heaven, they will inherit the earth, and they will be shown mercy (Mt 5:3–12). Like the early Christians, they hold all things in common (Acts 4:32–35).

The vow of poverty continues to have significance today, although in some parts of the world it presents challenges. In Asian nations plagued by grinding poverty, it seems incongruous that anyone could value poverty, much less make it the subject of a vow. In Africa the notion of private property is much less individualized than in the United States. Property belongs

---

[3] Sandra M. Schneiders, *Prophets in Their Own Country: Women Religious Bearing Witness to the Gospel in a Troubled Church* (Maryknoll, NY: Orbis Books, 2011); *New Wineskins: Re-Imagining Religious Life Today* (Mahwah, NJ: Paulist Press, 1986); *Selling All: Commitment, Consecrated Celibacy, and Community in Catholic Religious Life* (Mahwah, NJ: Paulist Press, 2001).

to the family and to the community. Missionary communities, with their vow of poverty, are more materially wealthy than the local populations they serve. This is true even if the missionaries themselves have lowered their standard of living radically in order to live among the people they serve. Even in the United States the vow of poverty could use some reimagining. Poverty may be seen as significant on three levels: the personal level, the community level, and the prophetic level.

On a personal level, the vow of poverty means that all we earn belongs to the community; we share all our goods in common. Yet all that we need comes from the common purse, whether basic needs of food, clothing, and shelter; education; retreats; or healthcare (canons 668, 670). In a deeper way the vow signifies letting go of the personal desire for all the latest in clothes, gadgets, experiences, and so forth. It involves a freedom from the accumulation of "stuff" that has become so prevalent in our society. It means the deliberate choice to simplify one's life, to have fewer things, to live more sustainably, to live lightly on the earth. This choice can be made by any Christian, and in fact, by any human being, but by making it the subject of a vow, religious make the choice to live it deliberately. Like everyone living in our consumerist society, we struggle with living out this choice, at some times more than at others. The vow of poverty gives us a context for reflecting on this choice and making it ever more a reality in our lives. The vow of poverty allows us to open extra space in our lives and clear away the clutter so there is more space for God, for community, and for mission.

On a community level the vow of poverty also affects the way people come together. We attempt to live in community the ideal of the fourth chapter of Acts when the early Christians held everything in common. We each do what we can for the support of the community, and we use what we need. In smaller communities that will be part of the future, the small, local unit can come together and pool its resources. Together, the group can take responsibility for the well-being of the group: Can we afford to send a member of the community to a low-paying or volunteer ministry? Can we afford to send a member of the community to continue her education? The group will make decisions as families do today. We will live in interdependence. Our personal value should not be based on what we have or on salary. In some cultures hoarding is considered a disease, whether it is hoarding stuff or power or money or honors. What we have, we have for all. This type of economy binds us together in interdependence. It challenges us to trust and to be trustworthy. If we have all chosen to pool all that we have, by that act we choose to trust and to be trustworthy. This requires mature commitment and periodic recommitment to the ideals. In medieval times, when individuals professed the vow of poverty, they were considered to be dead insofar as the law was concerned, incapable of owning or administering property. Over a lifetime this kind of living grows in depth and maturity. Religious life is my primary life commitment, and I give up a personal financial existence outside of the community; I give up stability and security of my own, independent of the community. The choice to bind ourselves together economically both symbolizes and facilitates our community, and it helps us act more and more interdependently. Economically, we stand or fall together.

On the prophetic level the vow of poverty helps to establish gospel-based sharing in community, and it can be an important witness in our society. Our world very much needs to hear the gospel message of simplicity of life, of living sustainably, and of sharing with those who have less. Holding all things in common, community members are able to support one another, showing that it is possible to live the gospel ideal that inspired the early Christian community. It is a witness to the world that there is enough, if only we are willing to share. If all people would share all that they have and use only what they need, we could solve the problems of poverty and world hunger. Economics of the community is not governed by self-interest, or the invisible hand of market capitalism, but by the invisible heart of love in a gift economy.

Obedience as Alternate Politics

The vow of obedience may have a longer history than the vow of poverty, having been an important part of Eastern monasticism and of the teachings of the fathers and mothers of the desert. In those lifestyles it was important to seek out a spiritual guide to learn the ways of religious life, whether lived alone in the desert or in a community. It was also explicitly professed since the beginning of Western monasticism. As with the vow of poverty, the vow of obedience had varying interpretations and spiritual meanings. Like Christ, who was obedient to God in all things, Christians sought to surrender completely to God. In this they placed great trust in a spiritual father or mother who could mediate the voice of God for them. As communities grew, obedience took on a communitarian dimension, facilitating the good order of everything. Saint Benedict opened his rule with the exhortation to listen:

> Listen, O my son, to the precepts of thy master, and incline the ear of thy heart, and cheerfully receive and faithfully execute the admonitions of thy loving Father, that by the toil of obedience thou mayest return to Him from whom by the sloth of disobedience thou hast gone away.[4]

Later in that same rule Benedict moderates the charge to obey the abbot by encouraging the abbot to listen to the members of the community, even the youngest, who also had much wisdom and insight into the ways of God:

> Whenever weighty matters are to be transacted in the monastery, let the Abbot call together the whole community, and make known the matter which is to be considered. Having heard the brethren's views, let him

---

[4] Benedict Verheyen, *The Holy Rule of St. Benedict* (Atchison, KS: St. Benedict's Abbey, 1949), Prologue.

weigh the matter with himself and do what he thinks best. It is for this reason, however, we said that all should be called for counsel, because the Lord often reveals to the younger what is best.[5]

The vow of obedience means that religious promise to obey their leaders according to their constitution.

The evangelical counsel of obedience, undertaken in the spirit of faith and love in the following of Christ, who was obedient even unto death, obliges submission of one's will to lawful Superiors, who act in the place of God when they give commands that are in accordance with each institute's own constitutions. (canon 601)

Communities have varied customs and practices regarding the vow of obedience, placing different emphases on the role of the singular leader and on the community gathered in discernment, and on the role of personal responsibility and dialogue.[6] Community leaders have been very gifted guides, and many have been much beloved by their communities and by wider society. However, over the course of history, there also have been superiors who fell prey to human weakness and became petty and arrogant, wielding autocratic control over their communities. This problem is as much about the insidious nature of power as it is about the natural human weakness of those called to lead. Other leadership has been unable to call the membership to its highest ideals and allowed communities to settle for a comfortable lifestyle, far short of the ideals to which they pledged themselves at the beginning of their religious life. Some interpretations of the vow have been militaristic, with a high value placed on prompt, unquestioning obedience to commands, based on believing that the superior speaks with the voice of God. At times the vow has been viewed in an

---

[5] Ibid., Chap. III.

[6] Amy Hereford, "Obligations and Rights of Leadership of Religious Institutes," *Religious Law and Consultation Newsletter* 124 (2012): 1–4.

overly juridical manner, with religious feeling justified in doing anything that was permitted, while silently daring leadership to deny any but the most egregious choices. Some interpretations of obedience have been very hierarchical, imbued with a particular masculine interpretation of power dynamics in community, leading to authoritarian styles of leadership. In the West, women's communities were placed under the authority of a male religious community or a bishop for most of the history of the church. Sometimes this authority was exercised with real pastoral concern, other times the women had to do their best to live their ideals despite external authority.

All of these various nuances pointed to the centrality of following Christ, who was obedient to death, and the importance of religious superiors in discernment of God's will. Today's understanding of obedience places a much greater emphasis on the full development of the human person and the development of a sense of responsibility and mutuality in decisions made by and for individuals as well as in decisions for the community as a whole. John Paul II writes:

> Obedience, practiced in imitation of Christ, whose food was to do the Father's will (cf. Jn 4:34), shows the liberating beauty of a dependence which is not servile but filial, marked by a deep sense of responsibility and animated by mutual trust, which is a reflection in history of the loving harmony between the three Divine Persons. (*Vita Consecrata*, no. 21)

Thus, individuals strive for a deep personal relationship with God, seeking to know and follow the leadings of the Spirit. They seek the call of God in prayer and contemplation, in the signs of the times, and in the events and circumstances of everyday life. Conversation with others in community or in spiritual direction and spiritual friendships also helps personal discernment. Those who know and love us can help us to be honest with ourselves and to explore the deepest truth found in our own prayer and insights. The personal movement is always one of surrender to

God's call, a call that leads each person to his or her truest self. This involves time and commitment, but even when the cost is high, it is also deeply rewarding.

We are moving from large provinces and congregations of a hundred or more members to smaller communities that may only have a dozen members and in which community discernment is much more intimate. In this new reality we come from a space of deep personal discernment into community in order to move together toward a discernment of the call of God in a particular situation. In this space of community discernment we encourage one another to come first from the space of deep prayer, and from our own truest self in love. When the community comes together, each one surrenders some personal autonomy to the group while retaining a responsible participation. This mutual commitment enables group discernment to unfold in an atmosphere of trust and mutual responsibility for the outcome. Each one shares in the struggle and commits to the outcome.

The prophetic dimension of obedience gives witness to decision making where each participant strives to be free of self-interest and looks instead for the common good, even at the expense of his or her personal interest. This requires a mature co-responsibility for the community and can be a tremendous witness to the gospel in view of the partisan political posturing of today's world.

Celibacy as Alternate Relationality

Historically, the focus of celibacy was the wholehearted giving of oneself to God to the exclusion of marriage, which is also a primary life commitment. The choice of celibacy was made to focus one's life on God alone and on the spiritual life. Saint Paul describes celibacy as freeing persons from the demands of family life in order to "be anxious about the affairs of the Lord, so that they may be holy in body and spirit" (1 Cor 7:34).

Parallel to the Old Testament portrayal of Israel as the bride of God (see Jer 3:8; Hos 2:16; Is 54:4–10), the New Testament writers described the church as the bride of Christ (see Eph 5:25–27; 2 Cor 11:2; Rv 19:7–9, 21:10). Taking up this imagery, early Christian writers described virgin-martyrs such as Saint Agnes, Saint Barbara, and Saint Lucy as brides of Christ. This imagery continued into the patristic period as an image for consecrated virgins and in the medieval period for women religious.[7] The vow of celibacy was seen as freeing women from earthly marriage to be available for heavenly marriage. This fostered a very personal mystical spirituality because women were also increasingly cloistered, completely isolated from the family and from the world of their day.

The vow of celibacy took on a practical significance in apostolic religious life. In the twentieth century, women's apostolic religious life was a place where women could give their lives in service, particularly in education and healthcare. This gave women the opportunity to excel in roles of leadership and to establish and expand large and effective institutions. They were able to develop their academic and professional skills in a way unprecedented for women in the history of the world. This was in part because they had pledged themselves to a life of prayer, community, and mission. This lifestyle included the vow of celibacy, which freed them from responsibilities for childbearing. In community, they were able to pool resources and share in responsibilities for the upkeep of the community. Women became very effective leaders in all the areas in which they worked.

Whereas the values behind the vows of poverty and obedience are common to all Christians, vowed celibacy is particular to the religious life and characterizes the lifestyle of religious. Single men and women are free to choose marriage or religious

---

[7] For the patristic period, see Philip Schaff and Henry Wace, *A Select Library of Nicene and Post-Nicene Fathers of the Christian Church*, vol. 4 (New York: The Christian Literature Co., 1892), 252. Saint Athanasius writes: "Speaking of consecrated virgins: Such as have attained this virtue, the Catholic Church has been accustomed to call the brides of Christ." For the medieval period, see Rabia Gregory, "Marrying Jesus: Brides and the Bridegroom in Medieval Women's Religious Literature," PhD dissertation, University of North Carolina, 2007, 15.

life. Spouses are committed to one another and to building a life together. Religious commit to remaining celibate in community, and this commitment colors the type of life that we lead. Bride of Christ imagery no longer speaks to most of those entering religious communities today. However, the commitment of celibacy does give a level of freedom to prayer, community, and ministry, without reference to a spouse or children. Our contemporaries may envy the freedom we have in this regard.

Coming into religious life, the vow of celibacy means that our primary life commitment is to the religious life. This enhances the ability of the group to trust in one another's commitment and the basic stability of the group. When we come into relationship with those outside religious life, celibacy affords us a freedom that enables us to come into relationships that are not overlayed with sexuality. This is not to say that sexuality never comes up. It certainly does. But celibacy settles our primary life commitment—as does marriage—and frees us for relationship in community and in ministry.

At a prophetic level celibacy points beyond this life toward union with Christ in God, the goal and purpose of all life (Eph 1:3–14; Col 1:15–20; 3:3). At the same time, in the midst of everyday realities, celibacy points us to a deeper spiritual experience of God and offers a witness to this life of union with Christ in God.

Framework for Gospel Living

The vows continue to be relevant for many of the same reasons they have always been relevant. However, as in every age before us, their relevance is colored by the context in which they are lived. For us today, the vows form the framework for sustainable, faith-based communities in which men and women commit their lives to God, to one another in community, and to mission. The perpetual commitment that we make to God and to our communities requires that there are others who are able to make this commitment and to sustain that commitment over a lifetime. Religious life is a stable form of life (canon 573). Though members come and go, and theology grows and develops, it is important that there be members who will continue to come so that there will be others among whom one can live a perpetual commitment. There is a benefit in cross-generational living in religious life. In the twenty-first century, for some communities this has come to mean that one working member lives in a semi-retirement or retirement community. This is not the most healthy arrangement. But when there is a balance among the generations, each generation can play a role among the others, and they all benefit from one another. People in their twenties and thirties are the parent generation in the wider society; they bring energy and innovation. Those in their forties and fifties are the grandparent generation in wider society; they bring leadership and productivity. Those in their sixties and seventies and above are the great-grandparent generation; they bring wisdom and stability.

Religious life requires a commitment and a surrender of some personal freedom and independent use of money, sex, and power. This commitment frees us for life together in community, sharing spirituality, and mission. For those called, this holds a strong attraction and is experienced as a deeply felt desire and call from God. Men and women who respond to this call today, with the challenging situation in many religious communities, feel this same deep call and high ideal for religious life, even though the present-day reality does not hold out the possibility of living the life they desire. Those in their twenties join a community whose average age is approaching eighty. This makes sense neither from a practical point of view, nor from the point of view of religious life, with the ideal of various generations supporting one another. Yet these men and women come, with a deep sense of vocation and a belief that a seismic shift is about to occur. Religious life will be dramatically different in the next ten to twenty years, and they feel called to be a part of what is emerging. Called to what is, they intuit the stirrings of what will be with a profound sense of wonder.

REIMAGINING COMMUNITY—
TWELVE MARKS OF NEW MONASTICISM

Women religious in their forties and fifties are increasingly calling for conversation on the future of religious life. This conversation acknowledges amazing developments in religious life over the decades since Vatican II and seeks to explore what will unfold in the next fifty years. In one such conversation circle, the members used the insights of the contemporary, faith-based, intentional community movement, self-identified as New Monasticism, following the insights of Dietrich Bonhoeffer discussed in Chapter 2. This invitation went out to gather women into conversation:

> Do you sense the urgency to commit yourself to the future of religious life as it is emerging today? Do you find yourself longing for community life that energizes you for mission? At the Giving Voice gathering this summer, a group of us sisters in our 40s and 50s felt a new energy stirring among us, and expressed a desire to continue the contemplative process and conversation, moving into action. Responding to this desire we invite you to participate in a process beginning this Advent and running through Pentecost.[8]

The group used the twelve marks of New Monasticism, developed by faith-based intentional communities as a framework for its discussion.[9] New Monasticism comes out of the evangelical tradition, and its members have sought to live together in gospel-oriented communities. In 2004, several of

---

[8] This invitation was drafted by Kristin Matthes, SNDdeN, and Amy Hereford, CSJ, and was circulated among women religious from the Giving Voice list and in various online circles and forums beginning on the first Sunday of Advent, November 2011, and running through Pentecost, May 2012.

[9] Rutba House, *School(s) for Conversion: Twelve Marks of a New Monasticism*, ed. Rutba House (Eugene, OR: Wipf and Stock Publishers, 2005).

these faith-based intentional communities gathered to explore the commonalities among the communities and share insights and experience. This gathering developed the twelve marks that seem to be common to many of the communities. These marks may be seen as a contemporary experiment in religious life that has neither the blessing nor the burden of two thousand years of experience. It was the task of some of the great founders of religious life to take the lived experience and reorient it, setting it in a more dynamic relationship with church and society and with the needs of their day. Those of us who are the heirs of two thousand years of collective experience in religious life can benefit from the fresh insights of this modern movement, which seeks to incarnate radical gospel living here and now. If some of the great innovators in religious life were present today, might they come to some of these same insights?

Those called into conversation were invited to a three-step process of contemplation, conversation circles, and an online forum. Every two weeks they took up one of the marks and brought it to personal prayer, holding it gently and listening deeply to God and the stirrings in their own heart. Sisters then gathered in circles, face to face, on Skype, or in other creative ways to share what was emerging around that mark. Circles organized themselves by region, religious family, or other networks. Finally, groups were invited to share a word, an image, or a stirring from their conversation. The prayer and conversations were rich and sustained. It was deeply moving to engage with others as the Spirit moved strongly within and among us.

In the occasional opportunity to share in a meal or a project at a local intentional community, we find elements of religious life in a new vitality: the common meal, sharing of prayer and faith, simple living, solidarity with marginalized communities, ecojustice, community gardening. This is a symbol of our sacramental triad of baptism, Eucharist, and penance enfleshed in the community that practices the simple triad of hospitality, meal, and reconciliation. These communities live many of these characteristics described in the twelve marks. In what follows I discuss each mark briefly, bringing out its importance for emerging religious life. For the sake of better understanding, I change the order of the marks. I organize them in three categories: contemplative dimension, relations within the community, and relations of the community to the wider world. These categories correspond to three commonly recognized elements of religious life: God, community, and mission.

Contemplative Dimension

First Mark: "Commitment to a Disciplined Contemplative Life"
This mark was particularly significant for the conversation because participants committed to the contemplative dimension of the conversation process. They committed to taking time and the space in their busy days and lives. In doing this, they also sought to understand the meaning of the commitment to a disciplined contemplative life for the future of religious life.

Prayer and contemplation are an absolute requirement for any committed Christian life, and they are certainly central to religious life. However, our lives have become so busy, so task oriented, so connected, that we have difficulty opening up a space for the Divine. This means more than dashing off a quick prayer on the way into a meeting or after hearing painful news. It means finding that quiet place, settling our mind, and quieting our soul. It means surrendering to God Who Is, to God who is Love. It means remaining in that posture and letting God recreate us in that divine image in which God first created us. It means saying yes to Love.

Contemplative prayer is a gift, and for many, perhaps for most, receiving this gift does not come easily. Receiving the gift of contemplation requires a certain definite commitment and discipline. It requires that we commit ourselves regularly to finding time in our busy schedules, to finding a quiet place in our noisy lives. It requires the discipline to stick with that commitment, but also the wisdom to know how to pursue this life in a healthy way. After all, God is also seeking us and reaching out in relationship. We can count on God to guide and reward our efforts. There are myriad resources on prayer, corresponding to the myriad ways God speaks to us and invites us into relationship. The particular commitment and the particular discipline may vary from person to person and over the course of a person's lifetime. However, it is always important that we make this commitment a priority. In communities, we can support, nourish, and challenge one another in our commitment to a disciplined contemplative life.

Relationships in Community

The next series of marks all relate to life within the community. The quality of life within the community will certainly affect relationships outside the community, so there is no absolute distinction. However, it seems that some of the marks are more focused on our lives together.

Second Mark: "Nurturing Common Life among Members of Intentional Community"

This mark seems to be "ripped from the headlines." Perhaps this is not the top story in *The New York Times* or the *Washington Post,* but it is a major theme in reports about what young Catholics and Christians are seeking, particularly what younger religious are seeking. A recent Center for Applied Research in the Apostolate (CARA) study on vocations to religious life in the last ten years finds that community is high on their list of priorities.[10] In addition, volunteer programs for those in their twenties and thirties, such as the Jesuit Volunteer Program, the St. Joseph Workers, and the Mercy Volunteers, all include an intentional community component, and this is a strong drawing card for these programs.

In a recent proposal journalist Jamie Manson called women religious to open their tents and their community to lay ministers

---

[10] Center for Applied Research in the Apostolate (CARA), *Recent Vocations to Religious Life* (Washington DC: CARA, Georgetown University, 2009).

who want their support.[11] However, younger women religious are finding increasingly that these communities don't exist. Their options for finding community are to live alone or with one or two other sisters, or to live in retirement or semi-retirement communities. Many of these women religious in active ministry are looking for community, particularly for vibrant communities that are mission focused.

We are in an in-between time when the communities that sustained religious life for the last fifty years are becoming smaller, and many of them are now retirement communities. But at the same time there is an increasingly expressed desire on the part of religious in active ministry for vibrant communities, communities that are very intentional about gospel living and that nurture and support the members for mission. Young people are gathering in these communities, and younger religious are also trying to form these communities among themselves. Often they reach outside their own congregation to find sisters who want to build these communities and have the passion and energy to do so. They do this for mutual support, but also with a sense that they are a part of a larger movement emerging within religious life, a movement that has the potential of a radical reimagining of the life and its future. This reimagining will put it squarely within the long and inspiring tradition of religious life, but also in deep connection with the highest hopes and dreams of today's world.

Living in community, we can support one another in our commitment to a disciplined contemplative live, in our sharing of community, in our commitment to ministry, and in our desire to balance the elements of prayer, community, and mission. Our lives have tended to become more and more busy as we try to keep up with all the demands of community and ministry, with fewer hands available to help out. It's time to work toward a balance.

---

[11] Jamie Manson, "The Future of Religious Life and the Plight of Young Adult Catholic Women," *National Catholic Reporter* (October 27, 2011), online edition.

In today's society we have grown accustomed to work that takes us out of our household living situation. In a community of five to ten people, the members may scatter in many directions for their ministry; they may follow different daily work schedules with different commitments outside work hours. This is in contrast to the early twentieth century, when the most common model was for sisters to live in a single house and all work in the same school or hospital, which was within walking distance. This difference can have a significant impact on the communities of today, enriched by the diversity, yet somewhat scattered by the many demands on the time and energies of its members. It will be an ongoing challenge to balance the business of ministry with the important needs of supporting one another in community and nourishing a personal life of prayer.

Commitment to a common project is one way to ameliorate this scattering effect of ministry. The group may become involved in one of the ministries where members work, offer ongoing assistance to a local parish or nonprofit, or work in a neighborhood sustainability project. This is not to add another commitment to already busy schedules. Instead, it is a way of building the cohesion of the community and allowing the community as a group to offer some service to the wider community. It could also enhance the visibility of the community and its witness to the values its members share.

Third Mark: "Geographical Proximity to Others Who Share a Common Rule of Life"

This mark is a further development of the notion of common life in intentional community. An intentional community of religious women shares prayer, meals, relaxation, responsibility for the community; and the various tasks of cooking, shopping, cleaning, paying bills, and all the myriad duties that go into keeping a home running. They learn to balance these community responsibilities with their ministry commitments and the various other responsibilities that they have taken on. Community can be a place for helping one another to balance these things in a world that tends to make increasing demands on us.

Geographical proximity enhances these communities, for example, when ministries are close to home or when various responsibilities in the community and church are close to home. It can also be helpful when other intentional communities are in the same area, because they can provide mutual support. As others join the group, they can become a web of communities that can provide assistance and hospitality. Religious communities who provide hospitality to members who are traveling include Catholic Worker houses and L'Arche communities.

Geographical distance has hampered some efforts to form emerging religious communities. Members of the same congregation are spread geographically, and each member is deeply rooted in her locale with friends, family, and relationships, and with professional licenses and ministerial networks. Social media and other electronic means have allowed communities to form at a certain level on the Internet. But there is, in the end, no substitute for sharing daily life together in the religious life that is emerging.

The New Monasticism shares its insight about the need to relocate closer to one another, in shared living space or within walking distance, in order to facilitate mutual support, intentional community, shared meals, shared prayer, and shared ministry projects.

In religious life some congregations are spread across the United States or around the world, and yet in any one area may not have enough active religious to build vibrant local communities. At the same time, in the same city, there may be a dozen or so religious of various communities who do not share life together because of relations with their own congregation of origin. Increasingly, these active religious are talking about the need to form vibrant communities in their local geographic region. These communities may have members from several congregations, each of whom retains a relationship with and responsibility to her home congregation. These sisters gather with a strong commitment to religious life, to community, and to ministry. Together they can build the kind of community that will sustain them over a lifetime and also will be a blessing to those among whom they live and work, as well as to their communities of origin.

Those urgently wishing to commit themselves to the future of religious life as it is emerging today long for communities that will energize them for mission. We have to find ways to begin to build them in our local geographic regions while still remaining connected to the congregational and inter-congregational networks that have nourished and sustained religious life to this point. As we gather in these new communities, we will begin to build something new, and I believe these communities will also be attractive to those who are seeking religious life today. When these women seek to join us, this movement in religious life will continue to unfold. We will begin to see that future expressed in Jeremiah: "For surely I know the plans I have for you, says the Lord, plans for your welfare and not for harm, to give you a future with hope" (Jer 29:11).

Fourth Mark: "Support for Celibate Singles alongside Monogamous Married Couples and Their Children"

This mark comes out of the evangelical tradition and its New Monasticism movement, with their emphasis on traditional families. When religious women take up this mark, we find ourselves drawn in two directions. First, we acknowledge the richness of various levels of community we share with all God's children, in traditional families and in the diversity of configurations of modern families and communities. Second, we value our specific call as celibate religious in the midst of the Christian community. More than any other element of religious life, celibacy distinguishes consecrated life from other forms of gospel living. It frees us for a particular way of living the gospel. It creates a particular space for a lifelong commitment to community and ministry. It colors our spirituality and our way of relating in community, in ministry, and in the world at large.

For us, this mark is an invitation to reflection about community and boundaries. Those in the intentional community movement have recognized through experience that there is an inverse relationship between inclusivity and sustainability. We can be all-inclusive, but if we lack boundaries, our identity loses focus and energies are dissipated. Modern community movements that have staying power have figured out how to build a *community of communities* that can be clear about identity and boundaries, allowing this clarity to strengthen their capacity for relationship with others. In today's world, religious communities have to meet their own need for intimacy, for boundaries, and for identity, balancing this with the call to hospitality and inclusion. Women's communities have moved away from the almost complete isolation of the cloister and must regain a sense of balance regarding community and boundaries.

In nearly every age and place where religious life has flourished, it has been a blessing to those who live it, but it has also been a blessing to the community of faith and to the wider society. One of the gifts it offers to the community of faith is that of a group of people who have made a definite public commitment through vows. That commitment of fidelity to a way of life can be a source of support and nourishment for the faith and spirituality of the wider community of faith. This can be seen in a real way in the increasing number of lay associates and other groups that are gathering with religious communities to share in their spirituality and mission. Communities have sometimes had questions about the appropriate level of involvement and the appropriate boundaries with associates and other groups.[12] This issue is likely to need more attention at this time of transition when the number of vowed religious continues to decline. Will associates and other aggregated groups find the internal cohesion and leadership to sustain themselves as religious life becomes a much smaller reality? Currently, many of these groups are strongly supported and nourished by their religious communities. Will the associate and aggregated groups become sustainable in a decade or so when the communities are no longer able to sustain them as they did at the beginning?

---

[12] See Amy Hereford, "Associates of Religious Institutes: A Way Forward," *RCRI Bulletin* 7 (2012): 4–20.

In the long history of religious life, there have been religious communities that had men, women, and families closely associated with them. To last, they have to find a way of balancing appropriate boundaries for the particular groups while at the same time building nourishing relationships among the groups. Religious families then become a community of communities that has a particular responsibility for building a vibrant and life-giving community within the immediate group. As each community attends to its own internal affairs, it then relates from a position of strength to other communities that may have a different focus and lifestyle. A community might consist of communities of vowed religious, families, volunteers, lay ministers, teachers, theologians, healthcare providers, and younger discerners. Each of these groups is at its best when it is internally sustainable. But with the mutual relations in the community of communities, it can gain further strength and support.

Fifth Mark: "Intentional Formation in the Way of Christ and the Rule of the Community along the Lines of the Old Novitiate"

This mark is a little startling to newer members of religious communities, for whom the words *old* and *novitiate* don't seem to belong together. Several thousand men and women have been through "intentional formation" in novitiates across the United States in recent decades. It is interesting to notice that the faith-based, intentional community movement is turning to the notion of novitiate as a guide to bringing new members into the community. The foundational group comes together and spends time discussing its values and refining a common vision for the community. Often this vision is written down in the form of basic covenants. Then, over time, that original vision grows and develops as the vision is shaped by the realities of daily living.

In today's society community living is much less common than it has been in the past. The twenty-first century is marked by individualism and materialism, and along with this, there tends to be a high degree of loneliness and isolation. This is happening at a time when our ability to connect electronically is at an unprecedented high. In this world the move toward community takes a deliberate choice and commitment. In religious life, as our numbers diminish, we find ourselves in smaller and smaller communities, then sometimes, despite our wishes, we end up living alone, like so many of our contemporaries. Many in the younger generations of religious and those coming to religious life in the early twenty-first century are seeking community and the commitment to mutual support in their spiritual lives. In community we can support one another as we seek to live simply, in harmony with one another and with all creation.

Because this is not the way of life of many of our contemporaries, formation for religious life lived in community will continue to require a deliberate period of orientation. However, it may be different from the formation plans that have developed over the recent decades. Formation for prayer, community, and mission will take place within the small local communities in which the religious life is lived. Spiritual and theological formation will allow members to continue to deepen their prayer life and learn the particular richness of the vows and consecrated life. Personal and human development give members insight into community living and into gospel-based service in ministry. Formation for mission will include professional preparation as well as an orientation to theological reflection and the spiritual resources needed to sustain a lifetime of service. Local communities will have to take responsibility for providing this formation, and the networks of communities will support one another in this important aspect of life. (This will be discussed in more detail in the next chapter.)

Sixth Mark: "Sharing Economic Resources with Fellow Community Members and the Needy among Us"
Sharing economic resources allows members to live in interdependence. Society teaches us to live independently and to be self-reliant. We learn this lesson well, and we accumulate the

possessions necessary to sustain our independent existence. Our culture teaches us to have more—more clothes, more gadgets, more tools—and to have the latest of each of these. In community we can begin to reverse this trend as together we commit to a life of simplicity and to sharing our resources so that we all have what we need. All that I have, all that I earn, goes into the community purse. We meet our needs through these shared resources. And through this commitment, we are able to share resources with those at the margins of society.

This choice to share resources touches our vow of poverty, which is lived in different ways in different communities. Religious institutes may have emphasized detachment, dependence, and asking permission. As we come into the twenty-first century, other values may receive more emphasis, such as simplicity of life, sustainability, and pooling resources to allow sharing with the poor. We offer one another the gift of freedom from accumulating goods.

Interdependence is a way of life in which we share all that we have and use what we need. All that I bring and all that I use affects those with whom I share life. I cannot independently decide to change jobs, seek education or enrichment, move out of the community, or make a commitment to service without pay. All these choices affect my community. Together we can seek the good of the group and also seek to free the group's resources for others. My economic choices do not separate me from others, but rather unite me to my community and also to the needs of the wider society in which we live. We can support one another in our choice to live simply and share generously. This is a lifelong journey as we learn to trust one another and to be trustworthy partners.

Seventh Mark: "Peacemaking in the midst of Violence and Conflict Resolution within Communities along the Lines of Matthew 18"
Peacemaking is a gospel call that comes to us on many levels. We are called to quiet our restless hearts and minds, to settle our lives, and to seek to live lives of peace and equanimity. Our

world pulls us in many directions, so that this isn't always easy; it is a lifelong quest.

The next movement is toward peace within our communities. Matthew teaches us that if our sister sins against us, we should go and tell her her fault, and keep it between the two of us. If she listens, then we have won her over (18:15–20). Further, we have built up our community and strengthened our way of life. This takes courage and trust. It takes time to build a level of relationship among us so that we can feel safe enough to allow ourselves to be called forth in this way and where we love deeply enough to call others forth. We build this level of love and trust in our personal lives through prayer and contemplation. We grow in it together through our lives in community, through practicing open and honest communication. We also build this up through our failures, through forgiving and being forgiven, through sharing the struggle together.

The movement from interior peace to community peace-building flows out to a world in need. Our society is marked by conflict and violence at many levels. Spiritual restlessness and lack of meaning lead to suicide and violence, to drowning oneself in consumerism, mind-numbing media, and adventures that fail to satisfy. Each of us is created in the image of God who is Love. Our hearts are made for God, and we are restless until we find our way to this God, to Love. Many people find their way to God through religion and spirituality, or find God in everyday things, in beauty and service and in reaching out in love to others. We can be peacemakers by sharing our own interior peace with others who seek this path. There will be times and moments when people will ask this of us, and we can share it freely.

We are called to be peacemakers in a world of violence (Mt 5:9). Our deep and honest living in community, sharing our gifts and resolving our differences, can be a way of living as peacemakers. It can also give us the skills to begin bringing peace to our neighbors, neighborhoods, parishes, and places of work. Living as peacemakers, building lives of peace, and knowing the struggles of peacebuilding in community make us authentic witnesses of the gospel and prophets of peace in a world broken by the pain of hatred, separation, and violence. We come to this task not as experts but as pilgrims committed to the way of peace. We have been captivated by the Prince of Peace and the gospel of peace. We become willing prophets of peace in a world sorely in need of it.

The marks we have examined thus far have brought us from the personal commitment to a disciplined contemplative live, which is the essential starting point of intentional community, to the various marks of life in community. Even here, we have seen that personal contemplation and life in community have an outward focus. In the next section we examine those marks with a deliberately outward focus and describe the community in relationship with the wider world.

Community in Relationship

Eighth Mark: "Care for the Plot of God's Earth Given to Us along with Support of Our Local Economies"

A major focus of faith-based intentional communities and of religious communities over the centuries is the care of the earth, local agriculture, and building a sustainable community. Many religious communities have had farms or large gardens that provided sustenance for the community and for its neighbors. This practice is coming back into popularity, as may be seen by the increase in local gardens, community-supported agriculture, and urban farming. Communities make a commitment to care of God's creation, and this commitment nourishes and sustains their lives together in several ways and nourishes and sustains their relationship with the wider community at the same time.

First of all, there is a spiritual value to caring for the earth. Gardening is good for the human spirit, particularly the contemplative dimension. Many contemplative communities have chosen gardening and agriculture as one of the means of sustaining the community. Working close to the earth and close to nature is a value, as are the fruits this work bears for the community. One reason for this is the fact that the scriptures are replete with images from nature and from farming. From the farmer who sows the seed, to the shepherd caring for the sheep to the hired workers in the vineyard, the images of the gospel come from nature rather than from cyberspace. Certainly we can find God in technology and cyberspace, but these are not the images of biblical times.

A second value of care for creation and support of local economies is the importance of living more sustainably. Our world has been increasing in complexity, and there is a seemingly endless stream of new conveniences. In the twenty-first century we can get exotic foods grown in distant places and hi-tech devices that connect us around the globe and plastic molded into every imaginable shape to assist and to amuse us. But we obtain each of these at a cost. Eating locally grown produce may limit our diet somewhat, but we avoid the environmental and economic cost of shipping foods over long distances. Choosing to support local agriculture and local economies helps bring us into contact with our society and supports the people among whom we live.

In addition, there is a collaborative element in caring for the earth and supporting local economies. One of the advantages of the old agriculturally based monasteries is that there was generally work for everyone. And this work united the community as sisters and brothers worked together for the common good. Though not everyone is a master gardener or has a green thumb, there is generally something that everyone can do for the support of a community garden. With a little help most of us can learn to know which plants are weeds to be pulled and which are not. We can also help with watering and harvesting. Those more inclined to indoor tasks, whether by preference or for health reasons, can help with cleaning, peeling, and cooking. Everyone can be on hand to enjoy a meal of fresh, home-grown vegetables, and there may be enough to share with the needy as well.

Commitment to local economies reduces the carbon footprint and helps build relationships with neighbors. It takes time to investigate local businesses and find the stores that cater to local farmers and producers. We can allow the sense of wonder and gratitude to grow as we commit anew to receive and nurture the abundance of God's creation right here in our neighborhoods, in our yards. We can begin to care for the earth and be enriched by reconnecting with the earth and with our neighbors.

Ninth Mark: "Hospitality to the Stranger"

Hospitality has long been the mark of a Christian community, from Saint Paul, who reminded the early Christians that by welcoming the stranger they might be welcoming angels (Heb 13:2), to the desert hermits, who welcomed those who sought their counsel, to Benedict, who taught his followers to show hospitality to guests,[13] to the Houses of Hospitality of the Catholic Worker communities. There is something deeply spiritual and deeply challenging about welcoming the stranger.

In order to be authentic, we must first welcome one another into community and build a space that is warm and hospitable. There are religious who feel that they are increasingly strangers in their own communities, and we have a responsibility to reach out to these men and women who have dedicated their lives selflessly and are not finding the support they need to sustain their lives of prayer, community, and mission. One sister spoke of the challenge of continuing to live her active religious life when her entire community moved to a retirement home. For the elders, it was appropriate, but the active sister found it challenging to maintain her relationship with the community while still meeting her own needs for companionship with those her own age. Many sisters long for vibrant local communities where they can live the adventure of religious life among their peers. In gatherings of religious in the younger age cohorts, the conversation quickly finds it's way to the challenges of being a stranger in our own communities, though we live with our own sisters and love them dearly. Too many are walking away from religious life out of frustration, while still believing in the life and still believing

---

[13] Verheyen, *The Holy Rule of St. Benedict*, Chap. LIII.

in their call to this life. Can we support one another through this challenging time as we reimagine religious life and build the communities and networks that will support it?

At the same time we feel the call to gospel hospitality toward those alienated by the various systems of power, those struggling to live with dignity in systems of injustice, those leading lives of quiet desperation, those who are "other" to me in many ways. Many communities commit themselves to active hospitality. Some are able to invite others to their own table on a weekly or monthly basis. Others share in the work of a local Catholic Worker house, soup kitchen, or L'Arche community. Hospitality to the stranger is a way of breaking down barriers. Many have recognized that the work of justice is advanced when we make an effort to get to know the poor, the imprisoned, the disabled. We discover the injustice in our own hearts and our complicity in systems of oppression. We are challenged to live in places where we can offer hospitality to those who cannot offer it in return. This challenges how we live, with whom we live, and where we minister. We have to come to grips with the enormity of the inequities in our society, and yet find hope and courage to contribute our loaves and fishes.

Tenth Mark: "Lament for Racial Divisions within the Church and Our Communities combined with the Active Pursuit of a Just Reconciliation"

Confronting our own racism is an important challenge. In confronting our own assumptions, we have to break out of our comfort zone before we even realize we have the assumptions. Our ministry choices often have underlying effects of racism, even if we are also motivated by practicality or good steward-ship. For example, how many of our communities have pulled out of low income and inner city ministries while maintaining our presence in more affluent areas that match the ethnic profile of the community?

In addition to ministry choices, how do racial divisions affect our communities? Most religious communities have continued to remain ethnically homogeneous. Very few have been successful in welcoming men and women of color and of various ethnic minorities into their midst. Religious institutes today are much more diverse racially, physically, and culturally than they have been in the past. However, much work remains to be done. This is a complex issue, because we cannot simply assume that *they* of diverse ethnic and racial backgrounds should come to *us.* We should welcome all those who come to us, particularly those who wish to join us. In addition, can we make it a point to go to areas where the racial and ethnic profile is different from our own? Learning languages and cultures that are different from our own can be a very helpful way to come to know what it feels like to be the minority. It does not wipe away white privilege, but it can be a way to start deconstructing our stereotypes.

In addition to confronting racism, we can also challenge ourselves to confront the other "-isms" of our society. We can learn when and how various unjust systems of power are at work and how we are complicit in maintaining the status quo by our everyday choices. One part of social justice goes out and confronts systems of power outside us. Another part of justice is to examine our own hearts and lives for the ways we support and profit from these systems of injustice. In community we can support one another in making the conscious choice to withdraw our support and to forfeit our profits from these systems. As we begin to live more just lives ourselves, we can be more effective witnesses and prophets to the justice proclaimed by the gospel.

Eleventh Mark: "Humble Submission to Christ's Body, the Church"

We have the image of the community of the first Christian century played out before our eyes every year in the readings of the Easter season from the Acts of the Apostles: energy, passion, amazement, radical commitment to gospel, community, and mission. We also have images of a little infighting as the story unfolds, and that's part of the reality too. Perhaps it's not accurate to call this the church; it is instead the Christian community. *Church* conjures up something much more formal than what existed in those early days. When I consider this image, I ask what "humble submission to the church" means to the resurrection community?

The church is the *ecclesia*, the community, the people who are called together, the people who are assembled, the people who are living the gospel. This church has a mutual responsibility to stay in communion, to listen, and to work for the building up of the whole of Christ's body. This call to communion requires many things of us, individually and as a group. Humble submission to this church requires that we be mystics and prophets of the God of love, that we lead lives of integrity, and that we speak the truth to one another in humility and in charity.

Throughout the history of the church individuals and groups within the Christian community have struggled to stay united. Whole churches have broken away from one another, each deeply committed to a particular gospel ideal, yet also struggling with how to square humble submission with integrity and fidelity to a gospel call. Communities have split over ideology and vision; theologians have been silenced or walked away from the church. Saints have been burned at the stake and have been excommunicated, only later to be exonerated and canonized. Sordid scandals and power mongering have marred the history of the community. Yet through it all, the words of Jesus' prayer have haunted the community of faith. In a powerful plea to God during the last supper, Jesus prayed that we might be one, one in Christ, as Christ is one in God (Jn 17:21). And so despite our differences, despite our failings, despite the challenges, we struggle for the humility to be a reconciling presence in the community of faith.

Humble submission to the church calls us outside our comfort zone, outside our circle of friends, outside our own community, with its particular insight into living the gospel. We are called to be in relationship with other Christians, with other people of faith, with others who seek to live the gospel, even when they differ from us, perhaps especially when they differ from us. We struggle to stay in relationship, and we struggle to stay at the table when it would be easier to walk away. We find the strength to be faithful to the gospel call to unity in our commitment to a disciplined contemplative life. We bring our divisions, our anger, and our frustration to the God of love, the God who calls us to be one. Together in community we challenge one another to the humility of this mark, the humility to submit to Christ's church with integrity and to call others in the church to the same.

Twelfth Mark: "Relocation to the Abandoned Places of Empire"
The final mark that we discuss here is actually the first mark in the traditional listing. It challenges us to move. It is like the words of Jesus to the rich youth to go, sell what he has, give to the poor, and come, follow Christ (Mk 10:21). This following will not bring us to the halls of power or to a life of comfort and leisure. It will bring us to the places abandoned by the rich and powerful; it will bring us to the fringes, to the margins.

Empire is used in this mark to refer to the systems of power and oppression, the opposite of gospel community. Empire has abandoned the innercities and the rural areas. These are the areas where we can gather communities precisely because they have been abandoned by the moneyed, the propertied, the powerful interests. This is the way of the desert fathers and mothers and of modern intentional communities. Relocation to the places abandoned by the Empire has been described as "a powerful liturgy of conversion and commitment;"[14] it is a journey into the heart of God.

By relocating to areas abandoned by Empire, we let go of the securities it offers, often illusory securities. As the authors of the Declaration of Independence stated when they threw off the bonds of Empire, "We mutually pledge to each other our lives, our fortunes, and our sacred honor" (para. 5). The choice to relocate to the margins is available to us because we have a certain

---

[14] House, *School(s) for Conversion*, 22.

power and the means to make this choice. But we use our power and our means to make the choice to stand in solidarity with the poor and marginalized. Together we can take a risk to live less securely and less comfortably. This choice makes it easier to live out our values because we are less beholden to the systems of power. We can choose sustainability; we can choose simplicity in order to live in relationship with those who are at the margins not by choice but by necessity, with those who have become the refuse of Empire's insatiable appetite for more.

Together, in community, we make the choice to relocate to the areas abandoned by Empire. And we can do this out of a gospel call and sense of justice. Our choice is supported by community members who share the same values and the same commitment. We give one another the courage to make this choice when we mutually pledge ourselves to this way of life. Perpetual commitment is part of religious life. It is true that not everyone who professes vows remains in religious life. Nevertheless, the quality of a lifelong commitment is important to religious life. There may be others with various commitments associated and aggregated to religious life. But the genius of the life requires that some are willing to make a lifelong commitment. And because others are willing to make that commitment, I have the courage to make it myself. The challenge of relocation galvanizes the response to God's call, the personal commitment to a way of life, and the mutual support that we offer to one another.

REIMAGINING MISSION— INCARNATING THE GOSPEL HERE AND NOW

Mission is integral to living the gospel. This is because mission is integral to God. God is love, and love, by its nature, goes out of itself toward the other. We are created in God's image, created in the image of love. This is our own deepest truth. So each of us is by nature missionary, oriented to the other, and to the good of the other in love. Mission means going out in love to live the gospel, preaching and "baptizing them in the name of the Father, and of the Son, and of the Holy Spirit" (Mt 28:19). It involves going out in love, with prophetic speech and actions, and in an attitude of dialogue and mutuality.[15]

Ecclesial Context

The task of reimagining mission in religious life begins with an exploration of the nature of the community that is sent. There has been a major shift in the ecclesial context due to theological, cultural, and sociological changes. However, as we live in the midst of accelerating change, it is sometimes difficult to notice its combined effect. And as we approach this task from different generational perspectives, it is important to name the changes, so that we are responding to the world as it is, not to the world as we imagine it must still be.

The ecclesiology of Vatican II, like so much of the council's import, is subject to various interpretations.[16] The church is best seen as a harmony of opposites. "Like all living realities it develops, it changes . . . and yet in the very depths of its being it remains the same; its inmost nucleus is Christ."[17]

It is a mistake, I think, to expect to find a fully coherent, systematic, and comprehensive ecclesiology in the conciliar documents. . . . [*Lumen Gentium*, chap. 1] ends with an insistence that it is at once a holy community of faith, hope and charity and a visible structure, the mystical Body of Christ and a hierarchically endowed society,

---

[15] Stephen B. Bevans and Roger P. Schroeder, *Prophetic Dialogue: Reflections on Christian Mission Today* (Maryknoll, NY: Orbis Books, 2011), 9–10.

[16] See Joseph Ratzinger, "The Ecclesiology of Vatican II," *L'Osservatore Romano English Edition* (January 23, 2002); Joseph Komonchak, "Ecclesiology of Vatican II," Catholic University of America, March 27, 1999, available on the publicaffairs.cua.edu website; Walbert Bühlmann, "The New Ecclesiology of Vatican II," presented at the SEDOS Seminar, Rome, December 3, 1996.

[17] Romano Guardini, *La Chiesa del Signore* [The Church of the Lord], (Brescia: Morcelliana, 1967), 160. Guardini is quoted in Ratzinger, "The Ecclesiology of Vatican II," I-1.

> a spiritual community and a visible group, endowed with heavenly gifts and existing here on earth, at once holy and always needing purification, a church that subsists in the Catholic Church.[18]

Two lines of development that continue to spark dialogue regarding the nature of the church are the universal and local dimensions. The church is universal, all are called to holiness, yet Christians are "from every tribe and language and people and nation" (Rv 5:9). The tension between local incarnation and universal unity can be a source of challenge and misunderstanding. One might ask how the church can be both Roman and catholic, both universal and localized in a particular church.

Another important line of development in ecclesiology since Vatican II is the new emphasis on the laity. In the first half of the twentieth century several important lay movements began to spread throughout Europe, such as Cursillo, L'Arche, Sant'Egidio, and Focolare. In the United States the Catholic Worker movement also began to take root and spread.[19] Pius XII took note of these movements and encouraged them. On February 20, 1946, he said:

> Within the Church, there exist not an active and passive element, leadership and lay people. All members of the Church are called to work on the perfection of the body of Christ. . . . Lay believers are in the front line of Church life; for them the Church is the animating principle of human society. Therefore, they in particular ought to have an ever-clearer consciousness not only of belonging to the Church, but of being the Church, that is to say, the community of the faithful on earth. . . . They are the Church.

---

[18] Komonchak, "Ecclesiology of Vatican II."

[19] Brendan Leahy, *Ecclesial Movements and Communities: Origins, Significance, and Issues* (New York: New City Press, 2011), 9.

It is no surprise then that the Vatican Council took up the issue of the laity in its documents, in both *Lumen Gentium* and *Apostolicam Actuositatem*. For example,

> By reason of their special vocation it belongs to the laity to seek the kingdom of God by engaging in temporal affairs and directing them according to God's will. . . . It pertains to them in a special way so to illuminate and order all temporal things with which they are closely associated that these may always be effected and grow according to Christ and maybe to the glory of the Creator and Redeemer. (*LG*, no. 31)

Several times the documents emphasize the link between the mission of the laity and the temporal order. To a lesser degree the potential of the laity for working in the pastoral, teaching, and healing mission of the church is mentioned.[20] In the years since the council there has been a great expansion of the sense of mission among lay Catholics, not only in "engaging in temporal affairs," but also in the full range of works of the church. Schools and hospitals once staffed largely by religious are now run almost entirely by lay Catholics who are both professionally prepared and imbued with a deep sense of mission.

Parable of the Academy

The following is a true story that has been repeated many times over the years after the closing of Vatican II.

The Academy of St. Mary was founded in the nineteenth century by the Sisters of St. Mary. It served the poor immigrant population, providing both an education and the hope of a better life. In addition, the sisters were careful to teach Catholic doctrine, strengthen the faith life of the students, and provide

---

[20] For this link, see *AA* nos. 2, 4, 28, 29, 30, 31; *LG*, nos. 31, 35, 36, 37, 40. For the potential of the laity, see *LG*, nos. 2, 33, 35.

an atmosphere steeped in Catholic culture. All the sisters who taught in the school lived in the convent on the Academy grounds.

The Sisters of St. Mary followed the progress of the Second Vatican Council, and when the council closed, they took to heart its call to read and study the documents and to begin the important work of implementing its directives. Almost overnight, the age-old, rock-solid stability of the church seemed to spring to new life as the windows were opened to renewal. During the early turbulent years after the council, the sisters examined every phase of their lives in the light of that council and made much needed changes to their prayer, community, authority structures, and mission. The responses of the sisters to the changes ranged from reluctant to exuberant, with some eagerly rushing ahead and just as many lagging skeptically behind. The community had recently swelled in numbers, receiving the largest number ever to enter in several successive years; the median age of the community was in the forties. The council had mandated that everyone be involved in the renewal of the community and its constitutions. Drafts and proposals were made and revised, read and discussed over several years. For many the upheaval was too great, too much was changing, too little was changing, they lost their sense of direction and identity in the onrushing renewal. Many left, and fewer entered. Eventually, life settled to a new normality.

Throughout the renewal of the congregation, the sisters continued their ministry of education in the Academy. The Academy, meanwhile, had sought to renew itself, adjusting to changes in the liturgy and seeking ways of teaching the age-old wisdom of the gospel in fidelity to the newly articulated insights of the council. Fewer sisters were available, and lay teachers increasingly took their places alongside the sisters in classrooms. Over the years this trend continued, with highly committed, skilled, and experienced lay teachers filling the places of sisters who left the community, retired, or moved into other ministries where the needs were greater. The number of sisters in the Academy dwindled, though the head of the school was always a sister. Then came the day when there was no sister qualified for that position. Sisters retained positions on the board, but they knew that even this would soon be impossible as well.

As the Academy prepared for celebrations of the fiftieth anniversary of the opening of the Second Vatican Council, the faculty and staff was made up exclusively of lay professionals. Three sisters still volunteered part-time in the offices. Their presence was important to the faculty and staff as well as to the students. The last sisters moved out of the convent just a few years ago; it is now used to supply much-needed space for the Academy's programs. The Academy's celebration of the council might take on a bittersweet tone as it bids farewell to the sisters who founded and staffed it for 150 years. Yet this progression has embodied one of the fruits of the council. Its mission is now entirely the work of the laity. This is an important context for considering the mission of religious women.

Social Context

Many of the religious institutes of women in the United States today were founded in the nineteenth century. Some began with a few members of a European congregation who came to this country as missionaries. They came to meet the pressing needs of society and of the church. They founded hospitals and schools where none existed. They taught the children, healed the sick, cared for orphans. They did this in a world where the needs were enormous and there were few resources in church, state, and society to provide assistance. There were no lay ministers and few women in the professions.

During the life of the congregations founded in the nineteenth century, many changes occurred in the place of women in civil society. In the nineteenth century many school districts forbade the employment of married women.[21] Religious women were allowed to work in these positions, supplying a

---

[21] See, for example *Jameson v. Board of Education*, 74 W. Va. 389 (1914).

much needed labor force. Married women were deprived of property rights; the husband was the sole owner of all property till the later part of the nineteenth century. In the early twentieth century, women gained the right to vote. During the two world wars the need for the expansion of the defense industry led to widespread hiring of women in jobs formerly reserved to men.[22] After the war many women lost their jobs, but with the civil rights movement of the 1960s and the Civil Rights Act of 1964,[23] legal protection was afforded to women in the workplace, though there remains a "gender gap" in wages and treatment of women.

This context is an important backdrop to the task of reimagining mission in religious life. Women religious served the unmet needs in church and society in the nineteenth and early twentieth centuries, a time when there was no other way for these needs to be met due to social, cultural, and ecclesial realities. They also spent a lifetime in service and achieved educational and professional competence nearly impossible for lay women. These realities have changed. As we look at the field of mission today, we see an empowered laity and a society that is increasingly cognizant of the basic human dignity of each human person. There are certain fundamental human rights that have been recognized at the national and international levels. We still debate the responsibilities and economics of the issues, and as a society, we don't do enough to provide a basic standard of living to the weakest and poorest members of society. But we do have mechanisms in place to begin to provide this. The Catholic education system and the Catholic healthcare system are now staffed at all levels by highly dedicated and skilled professionals. Some serve out of a deep sense of mission as Catholics or other Christians. Others serve from a sense of personal and humanitarian commitment.

---

[22] Gerald D. Nash, *The American West Transformed: The Impact of the Second World War* (Lincoln: University of Nebraska Press, 1990), 221–22.

[23] Civil Rights Act of 1964, Pub.L. 88–352, 78 Stat. 241 (1964).

Reimagining Mission

Many of the religious congregations in the United States today were founded for particular apostolic works. Those works are now being carried out by others. The question for religious today is: What is the ongoing relevance of apostolic religious life in today's church and in today's world? What do small groups of committed men and women religious bring to mission, when they often serve as the only religious among their lay colleagues? Religious often serve in education, healthcare, pastoral care, or social service with single and married men and women and with clergy. Their colleagues are as well educated, as theologically prepared and as committed as they are.

Religious life is a stable form of life shaped by the vows, with a lifelong commitment to spirituality, community, and mission. Those coming to religious life today often come from the ranks of lay ministers in education, healthcare, pastoral care, or various forms of social work. They no longer come *for* mission, as they did in previous generations. They come *from* mission, seeking a deeper commitment to spirituality and the blessings and challenges of community. They seek the particular type of community formed by those who have made the serious personal commitment to vowed religious life. They seek to live the Christian mission in this context.

The central mission of religious life is the same as it has always been. It is for those called to this way of life to connect deeply with God Who Is, with God who is Love. Many come to religious life with their spirituality well developed. The years of formation that they spend before final incorporation into their communities should deepen and enrich their spirituality. This is the beginning of a lifetime that is more amply supplied with opportunities for prayer and spiritual development than that of our lay counterparts, and generally more than that of the secular clergy as well. Religious have opportunities for ongoing theological reflection on their lives in community, their shared commitments as a group, and their personal work in mission.

As we go forward, the life, community, and spirituality of religious will reclaim a center place in the sense of mission. We will drink deeply from the sacred wellsprings and surrender freely to the invitation of God to ever deeper union. Recreated by regular contemplative prayer, we must go forth in mission. Out of our contemplative stance, we must step out in prophecy. But it will rarely be prophecy of words. We will prophesy by coming into community, supporting and challenging one another's commitment. We will prophesy by doing the gospel in everyday life, by doing the works of God in education, healthcare, pastoral and spiritual work, and social service. Our church and our society do not need our big institutions or our labor force. Our church and our society need our commitment and the witness of committed lives lived in service of the gospel. We seek to live, as did the first Christian community, with our eyes fixed on the future restoration of all things in Christ (Col 1:20) and our lives committed to that purpose.

CHAPTER FIVE

THE NEW FORM OF RELIGIOUS LIFE

This chapter turns to practicalities of structure, governance, and formation for the emerging reality of religious life. The emerging life form will not need the infrastructure that has served the dominant cohort in the past century. That infrastructure was built for hundreds or even thousands of sisters staffing large institutional ministries. Those ministries are now in the hands of capable and committed lay people. Emerging religious life has the task of imagining the infrastructure that will support and enhance its life going forward. Likewise, it has the task of reimagining formation, exploring the ways in which newer members can be welcomed and integrated into this new life form that is smaller, more local, and more autonomous than religious life of the twentieth century.

GOVERNANCE: FROM HIERARCHY TO NETWORK

The trends in structure and governance come out of several contemporary cultural movements. Much of what has been said in previous chapters informs the response proposed here. But it is also important to look specifically at some cultural movements that affect the way people organize themselves today.

Postmodernism

Postmodernism is a term used by scholars in many fields as well as by those commenting on culture. It refers generally to the move from objective reality "out there" to subjective reality "in here." In literary criticism a text may be read through many lenses, and while there are certain objective aspects to a literary work, the interpretation also depends on where the critic stands in his or her historical, cultural, and philosophical perspective. Postmoderns acknowledge that we critique all of reality in this same way. Moderns would agree that our views of the world, of society, of government, and even of church and God are all colored by our perspective. Postmoderns go further and say that our world, society, government, and even church are all socially constructed.

We have observed a particular undermining of the structures of power. Although they remain in place, many structures have undermined their own credibility and authority. This time of breakdown is also characterized by a spontaneous regrouping around particular values of oneness, tolerance, collaboration, acceptance, and respect.[1]

We are emerging from a world in which there were dominant narratives about who and what are important and about the meaning of power. We are discovering that these so-called meta-narratives were illusions. They never spoke the truth of the majority, but instead embodied the dominant point of view that was white, Western, educated, landed, male, and clerical. This point of view was established as normative, the yardstick by which all others were measured and found wanting. It is said that postmoderns have subverted the dominant paradigm. Perhaps it is more correct to say that postmoderns see through the dominant paradigm and seek to subvert the paradigm of domination. They see the rich diversity of languages, peoples, cultures, and ideologies as a blessing to be celebrated, not chaos to be controlled. As this diversity is empowered, the richness of the single common human story comes through; we live, we breathe, we love, and we are loved, and we come into relationships, networks, and communities. Postmoderns have a

---

[1] André Maureen Soete, "A Vowed Response to the Postmodern World," *Review for Religious* 59, no. 3 (2000): 601, 607.

particular ear for minority stories and for the deconstruction of systems of power.

At the same time, postmoderns are able to organize themselves around meaningful centers and form overlapping circles of community and of influence. They are learning to include everyone in spheres of influence that honor each one's commitment, balancing inclusivity and hospitality with the boundaries necessary for a community's sense of identity, cohesion, and need for sustainability.

Emerging church is the name given to communities that practice the way of Jesus within postmodern cultures. This definition encompasses nine practices. Emerging churches (1) identify with the life of Jesus, (2) transform the secular realm, and (3) live highly communal lives. Because of these three activities, they are able to (4) welcome the stranger, (5) serve with generosity, (6) participate as producers, (7) create as created beings, (8) lead as a body, and (9) take part in spiritual activities.[2] *Emerging* catches into one term the global reshaping of how to "do" church in postmodern culture. It has no central offices, and it is as varied as evangelicalism itself. It reflects the collapse of inherited meta-narratives (overarching explanations of life). Why have they collapsed? Because of the impossibility of getting outside their assumptions. Those in the emerging church focus on praxis rather than doctrine, they critique the use and misuse of power, and they go out in mission in practical, local ways.

Occupy Wall Street

Occupy Wall Street and the hundreds of other occupy movements that it spawned are an example of postmodernism. Occupiers have no central governance, no hierarchy, and no gatekeepers ensuring a unified message. Yet the movement resonated in the hearts and imaginations of thousands across the globe. The current systems of power only remain in power

---

[2] Eddie Gibbs and Ryan K. Bolger, *Emerging Churches: Creating Christian Community in Postmodern Cultures* (Ada, MI: Baker Academic, 2005), 44–45.

because of the unwitting consent of those who value their meager comfort over the risk of taking responsibility for their lives and the life and well being of humanity and of the planet.

Occupiers "engage in direct and transparent democracy." They gather to build consensus on group action while at the same time empowering smaller action groups to develop and carry out their own projects. Occupiers "recognize individuals' inherent privilege and the influence it has on all interactions." Everyone has some power and influence. When we acknowledge our power, we are able to use it consciously and responsibly, and to moderate our power in order to allow those with less power to make their voices heard and make their needs known. Occupiers also seek to "empower one another against all forms of oppression."[3] This comes out of the group's orientation to personal responsibility for taking action on the ground to advance the cause of justice. While not negating the importance of legal action, it focuses on the power of personal responsibility and personal choice in building a more just society. Occupy is about small, self-organizing groups of committed people who imagine a more just society and then commit themselves to making it a living reality. They also subscribe to the following values: revaluing labor; individual privacy; education as a basic human right; and making technologies, knowledge, and culture accessible to all.

Occupy Wall Street and the many Occupy encampments across the country and around the globe have given a concrete witness to what postmodernism looks like in practice. They are willing to drop out of an unjust system in order to reimagine democracy and to reimagine a society in which resources are more equitably distributed.

Intentional Community

The sociological signs that are present in the twenty-first century will witness the dissolution of the hegemony of the classical

---

[3] These three Occupy principles are taken from the New York City General Assembly website, www.nycga.net.

paradigm of monasticism as a total institution. In its place will emerge flexible, eclectic, deregulated modes of postmodern religious life.[4]

The New Monasticism movement has come to embody this emergence with communities committed to living very intentionally, gathered to live lives that are spiritually meaningful, socially just, and environmentally sustainable. The members commit to certain practices, both individually and as a community. These communities do not generally have a rigid hierarchical leadership structure; sometimes they do not have any hierarchy or recognizable leadership structure at all. However, rather than being leaderless, they are "leader-full." Everyone takes responsibility for the leadership of the group. When this works well, the community has managed to find a balance between the need to involve all the members in important decisions and trusting individual members to make decisions in particular cases for the good of the group. It takes time to negotiate this balance, and the community must commit to taking the time to find this balance and, when necessary, to renegotiate it as things change.

Basil Hume, OSB, says this of the persistence of monasticism: "Destroy it in one age, it will reappear in another; drive it out from one nation, it will take root elsewhere; if it dies in one place, it will be reborn somewhere with an almost stubborn persistence."[5] It is easy to see the New Monasticism and the intentional community movement as a reappearance and rebirth of the age-old institution of monasticism. These communities have a fresh and thoroughly modern feel, while at the same time they seem to spring from the same spiritual DNA as all the great religious communities of the Christian era.

---

[4] William J. F. Keenan, "Twenty-First-Century Monasticism and Religious Life: Just Another New Millennium," *Religion* 32, no. 1 (January 1, 2002): 13.

[5] Basil Hume, *In Praise of St. Benedict A.D. 480–1980* (London: Hodder and Stoughton, 1981), 63.

Open Source

The principles of open source software development are post-modern. One example of open source software development is Linux, first released in 1991, a computer operating system developed through the collaboration of thousands of individual volunteers worldwide and made freely available to millions of users who download and install it on their computers. Linux developers and users form the Linux community, in which each contributes what he or she is able to the endeavor, and all are able to use the resulting software. In some ways this might be compared to the story of the "loaves and fishes"—each contributes a small amount, but when blessed by the collaboration of all, the multitudes are supplied.

Linux is the work of many people who have built on the earliest innovations in computing, dating back to the 1960s. Many developed components of the operating system with the idea that software should be free and available to all. In the 1980s the use of computers spread; they began to be used in homes and businesses for word processing and data processing. Microsoft and Apple developed commercial operating systems. During this time free software enthusiasts continued to develop and promote open source computing. Linus Torvalds, a Finish doctoral student in computer programming, contributed two crucial elements to the movement in 1991: software and a method for developing software. He developed a kernel, a key piece of software at the heart of the operating system, and posted his work on an Internet newsgroup. He invited others to add to what became the collaborative, community-driven, open source development method. Programmers from around the globe responded to the initial post, expressing interest in the project and offering suggestions.[6]

---

[6] See Linus Torvalds and David Diamond, *Just for Fun: The Story of an Accidental Revolutionary* (New York: HarperCollins, 2001), 85.

Open source development is community driven and the quality of the product depends on the network of developers and users along with the synergy of their collaboration. Open source is only a methodology; it is up to the community to produce the result. This method of collaboration encourages individuals to work on parts of the whole project and to make suggestions and create solutions to problems they see. A network of developers evaluates fixes and patches and implements them into the whole project. The Linux community has developed the capability to maintain a high level of integrity in the product and to balance new features with the need to maintain stability in the overall project.

Instead of locking the inner workings of the program behind layers of encryption, Linux freely offers the source code for examination and tweaking by every user. The newest high-school programming student can offer suggestions and fixes. Open source projects come to a certain level of usability, but in a sense they are open-ended projects; there is a sense of incompleteness and openness to improvement in every release. One value of the process is that it brings the users in close contact with the developers. As a community-driven project, Linux encourages and values the contribution of each person—programming, using, testing, and promoting the software. From the beginning, Torvalds facilitated the development of a broad network of collaborators and facilitated the movement of ideas and information throughout the network. Each one contributed not from a profit motive but in order to share his or her knowledge and to be enriched by the value created by all.

The Starfish and the Spider

Bookstores and Amazon always sport dozens of titles on the latest new management theory and the best strategy to get ahead, make money, and stay on top. However, there is also a growing literature on how to lead in a postmodern organization. Authors stress how to decentralize, flatten hierarchies, and support a sustainable economy that works for everyone. In Chapter 3 we discussed one such book, *The Starfish and the Spider*.[7] The book's title image embodies its central message. Some organizations are structured like a spider with specialized structures—a head that is in control and directs the operation of the spider. If you cut a leg off the spider, it is lame; cut off its head, and it dies. In contrast, the starfish has a circular neural network and all its functions are distributed throughout its arms. If you cut off the arm of the starfish, it grows another, and it has no head to cut off.

This decentralized structure is proposed as a model for organizations. For some organizations it is an invitation to decentralize. For other organizations it is simply a description of how they work and move ahead in today's world. It describes how the Occupy movement works and how intentional communities organize themselves. The authors also point to eBay, Wikipedia, and Craigslist as examples of decentralized, leaderless organizations that are nonetheless highly successful. They offer ten rules that come into play in these organizations, rules that are more descriptive than prescriptive.

"Rule 1. Diseconomies of Scale."

The principle of economies of scale refers to the efficiency and savings that can be realized by combining smaller organizations into larger organizations. Diseconomies of scale refers to the problems that cause these larger entities to become inefficient: communication costs, top-heavy administration, greater difficulty in responding to changing needs, and the well-documented phenomenon that individuals in larger groups tend to be less efficient.

"Rule 2. Network Effect."

New communication technologies allow individuals greater access to people, information, and resources than in the past.

---

[7] Ori Brafman and Rod A. Beckstrom, *The Starfish and the Spider: The Unstoppable Power of Leaderless Organizations* (New York: Portfolio Trade, 2008).

This enhances the power of the individual and the group, and can be exploited for the good of communities.

"Rule 3. Power of Chaos."
In highly organized systems, individuals and groups have to break through the systems of management in order to promote a new idea, product, method, or cure. However, in decentralized systems, any idea is as strong as those who are willing to develop it. If it works, they can promote it to those around them; if not, they move on to the next idea. Good ideas spread through the network. Some ideas are great for a few individuals, who adopt them. Others are free to choose other paths.

"Rule 4. Knowledge at the Edge."
Because of decentralization and the power of the network, all members have access to the knowledge necessary to refine their ideas and make them grow and flourish. Each person can also look around for others with consonant vision and join with them.

"Rule 5. Everyone Wants to Contribute."
While some enjoy being a cog in a wheel, studies also show that everyone enjoys being able to contribute to the overall goals of their organization or project. Smaller self-organizing groups allow for this.

"Rule 6. Beware the Hydra Response."
The hydra response is the ability for groups to break off and form their own organization, even in competition with the original group. This is acknowledged and even encouraged by the system; it keeps it vital.

"Rule 7. Catalysts Rule."
Catalysts are the critical drivers of the organization but not its leaders. Everyone in the organization is a leader. Catalysts are

the visionaries who propose new methods, ideas, and systems that inspire others and move them to action.

"Rule 8. 'Values' Are the Heart of Any Organization or Network."
The principle of cohesion is not structure or hierarchy but the values that inspire each individual. Because of the hydra rule, if individuals are not inspired by the vision and values of the organization, they can cut themselves off and reorganize with others of similar values. The new group may be an ally of the previous group, both working toward similar goals, but each organized around the goals that most closely align with those in the group.

"Rule 9. Measure, Monitor, and Manage."
Even in decentralized groups, basics of good organization are important.

"Rule 10. Flatten or Be Flattened."
Flat organizations are those without hierarchy. Christina Baldwin describes the flat organization as a circle with a leader in every chair.[8] In a small organization every person's commitment counts. Every person is in a position to make a difference. And every person is important in the life and work of the group.

No organization is completely centralized or completely decentralized, though most older and larger organizations are more centralized. And decentralized organizations may take on some elements of centralization in order to keep united and advance their goals. The key is to find the "sweet spot" between centralization and decentralization that is appropriate to the group and its organization.[9] Current shifts in culture and

---

[8] Christina Baldwin and Ann Linnea, *The Circle Way: A Leader in Every Chair* (San Francisco: Berrett-Koehler, 2010), 142ff.

[9] Brafman and Beckstrom, *The Starfish and the Spider*, 179.

advances in communication create an environment favorable to the shift toward decentralization, toward starfish organizations.

Thus far we have examined the way that late twentieth and early twenty-first century movements organize themselves. These organizations show an impressive instinct for self-organization, shared power, and distributed authority. But what does all of this mean for religious life?

EMERGING COMMUNITIES

Religious life arose through the Christian centuries when men and women set out to live the gospel with fresh enthusiasm and renewed vision. Led by the Spirit and imbued with a vision for living the gospel, they shared their inspiration, and others joined them to make it a reality in a religious community. Over time, these communities encountered the various forces of society, church, and state. Each of these forces shaped and molded the original inspiration. Over time these communities took on the structures that gave them more stability and permanence than they had when they first gathered. Structures must continue to evolve and adapt if they are to retain their vibrancy. Sometimes this can be done gradually and organically. At other time society continues to grow and change, and the community grows and changes as well; eventually, the structures may be come outdated and need more radical renewal or updating. An accelerating rate of change in the late twentieth and early twenty-first centuries has made it nearly impossible to keep pace in growing and adapting structures.

Today's smaller groups of religious can take inspiration from the various social movements around them. In fact, those coming to religious life today are likely to be "wired" differently than their elders who came to religious life in the mid-twentieth century. Gen Xs and Millennials have lived most of their lives in a postmodern world and have internalized its values. Admittedly, these values are both positive and negative. Their task is to use the positive values of postmodernism while trying to moderate the negative. Smaller self-organizing groups are more likely to succeed in the future.

At various times in the history of religious life, small, local communities have been very successful. There is also a trend in religious life toward centralization. For example, the Franciscan and Dominican orders maintained unity, particularly in the male branches, even as the orders spread from country to country. Both orders were founded as reform movements, and the unity was seen as a way to ensure that all members remained loyal to the founding principles. Friars professed vows in the order, with openness to being sent to any house of the order. This was in contrast to Benedictines, who professed stability to a particular monastic community. Later apostolic communities were also centralized, enabling them to coordinate hundreds of recruits in service of the group's missionary efforts. The megacommunities that resulted have made truly admirable strides in spreading the gospel and in addressing social needs. In the wake of Vatican II, religious made efforts to decentralize. Doing so will enable the next generations of religious to return to smaller, more localized, self-organizing communities.

It is interesting to note that while men's religious institutes retained a high degree of centrality, women's communities often broke into smaller local groups as they spread across the globe. Witness the countless women's congregations of Dominicans, Franciscans, Sisters of St. Joseph, and Benedictines. Historically, women's communities are much more likely to have split into local congregations than their male counterparts. This is in part due to the fact that through much of history, women's communities were required to be under the supervision of either a men's community or a bishop. Often, as women's communities spread, the local bishops sought to exercise control over the women's communities in their dioceses. Some groups split at the instigation of the bishop, who did not want "his" sisters answering to an outside authority. Other times the sisters sought independence from their distant founding community in order to have greater flexibility and ability to respond to local situations without waiting months for responses to arrive by letter from across the ocean.

The small, local groups of women were able to adapt to local situations and spread quickly in the developing American society. However, as the communities developed and came into contact with one another, there was in many cases a strong sense of isolation of one congregation from another. Only rarely did sisters from one congregation maintain ongoing community or ministry with those from other congregations. Today, it is much more common for religious to collaborate across congregational boundaries in formation and in ministry. Increasingly, they are considering inter-congregational communities as well.

With the advent of the Vatican's apostolic visitation of women religious in the United States, beginning in 2008, the collaboration among women religious reached a new high as they sought to study and respond to the questions put to them by the Vatican. The collaboration has brought into relief the many similarities among the various institutes, though they express their spirituality and mission in different terms. Religious are seen as part of a movement within the church and as strongly united among themselves. In this, religious life in the West has become more like religious life in the Eastern Christian Churches, where it has always been seen as a movement. In the East, religious life has remained a united movement, lived in various local communities. It never knew the division into various orders and congregations to the extent that was a reality in the West, particularly during the missionary expansion in the nineteenth and twentieth centuries. With its elements of decentralization, Eastern religious life gives a glimpse into where the structures of Western religious life may be headed.

Although the twenty-first century has witnessed a greater collaboration among religious women, the infrastructure that divides them into separate congregations and provinces remains. This infrastructure tends to isolate the groups of women, even as they face similar problems of aging, a smaller pool of candidates for community leadership, and dwindling finances. The answer to this dilemma is not collapsing all communities into larger and larger groups, but rather creative collaboration to enable sharing of resources and developing common solutions to common problems.

This will pave the way for younger religious to form small, local communities that are networked for mutual support rather than being established in a predetermined structure. The structures of religious life today have left aside much of the rigidity and hierarchy of the past; however, even the remains of these structures will probably not be helpful to the smaller groups that are emerging.

These smaller communities can take advantage of the strengths of each local community and be mutually supportive of the entire movement. They will all share the values of spirituality, mission, justice, and sustainability. But each local group will live these values in different ways, depending on the members within the community and their skills, interests, and the needs of the particular neighborhood in which they find themselves. "That post-French Revolution chapter of active religious life animated by the counter modern spirit of the Tridentine night battle is drawing to a close . . . and more ad hoc arrangements will be made."[10] In every age religious life has been the seed bed of evangelical innovation, meeting new needs in new ways while still integrating the tried and true wisdom of the ages.

Saint Benedict writes in his rule:

> But a third and most vile class of monks is that of Sarabaites, who have been tried by no rule under the hand of a master, as gold is tried in the fire; but, soft as lead, and still keeping faith with the world by their works, they are known to belie God by their tonsure. Living in two's and three's, or even singly, without a shepherd, enclosed, not in the Lord's sheepfold, but in their own, the gratification of their desires is law unto them; because what they choose to do they call holy, but what they dislike they hold to be unlawful. But the fourth class of monks is that called

---

[10] Keenan, "Twenty-First-Century Monasticism and Religious Life," 18–19.

Landlopers (Gyrovagues), who keep going their whole life long from one province to another, staying three or four days at a time in different cells as guests. Always roving and never settled, they indulge their passions and the cravings of their appetite, and are in every way worse than the Sarabaites. It is better to pass all these over in silence than to speak of their most wretched life.[11]

These restless wandering monks proved to be disruptive in Benedict's time and drew his contempt. Benedict proposed a remedy of stability and the ordered life of community. Self-gratification and indulgence of passions cannot be the basis of a new way of life. But the stability and order that he proposes must be humane and flexible enough to gather and nurture the deep evangelical desires of itinerant postmoderns.

William Keenan, who posits that postmodern religious life will likely give more place to "Sarabaites" and "Gyrovagues," proposes the following characteristics of twenty-first century religious life:

Borderless, globalised monasticism: cross-institute memberships

Eclectic, portfolio spiritualities: modularised ways

Customer-focus: monastic designer lifestyles

Time-limited religious 'adhocery': a life-stage approach

Deregulation: relaxation of Rules and de-centralisation of ecclesial control

Monastic marketisation: niche-marketing and brand-imaging

Dialectic of detraditionalisation and retraditionalisation

Monastic mergers: spiritual and apostolic alliances

Mixed-mode monasticism: lay-clerical flexibility

Online monasticism: virtual religious communities.[12]

---

[11] Benedict Verheyen, *The Holy Rule of St. Benedict* (Atchison, KS: St. Benedict's Abbey, 1949), chap. 1.

[12] Keenan, "Twenty-First-Century Monasticism and Religious Life," 22.

It will take genuine wisdom and vision to form these new communities in the creative chaos of present-day religious life. Confidence in the age-old wisdom of the gospel and its incarnation in generation after generation of religious are critical. This life still has the power to enchant and inspire new generations, if those currently living it have the courage to let them try and hold them lightly as they come into their communities. The communities that form will spontaneously network with other intentional community movements that share many of their values. It may take time for the movement to find its new form and to bring into it, from the storehouse of religious life, both the new and the old, in order to rebuild the life for the twenty-first century.

Community of communities is a term used by the intentional community movement. It refers to the notion that communities are small self-organizing groups, but that they often form a web of relationships with various other intentional communities having similar interests and goals. The individual communities clarify their vision and pursue their goals as a group. They maintain openness to other communities in their network who may be pursuing similar or complementary goals. Through a loose relationship of mutual support, they are able to enhance one another's communities, while at the same time remaining true to the vision that gathered and inspires each community and each member.

These new communities will be small and local and will not need the infrastructure that exists in many congregations today. They can rely on a growing network of communities to help support and sustain their life. Local religious communities can unite periodically and can network with other communities across the country and around the globe. These networks can be face to face and online.

As each community grows and matures, it will find itself in need of periodic renewal. As communities network, they can take from the history of religious life the custom of sending visitors to the various communities to help each community renew its life together, have the difficult conversations, and ensure that it is getting what it needs for its life and growth. The network can also explore those areas where centralized coordination could be useful. For example, the communities could have a travel directory so that traveling members might stay with a local community and share its life in a spirit of mutual renewal. Communities might also join to form cooperatives to provide the services that larger congregations are now providing to their members, such as formation, education, insurance, and healthcare.

We can imagine this movement will begin as women religious from various communities come together in their local areas to build community together. But as the movement matures, it is likely that others may wish to join. At that time the movement will have to begin to reexamine and reimagine formation. We can begin that process even now, because if there is one thing sure about the current state of religious life, it is that "what is" is not sustainable. Even those entering current religious communities should be prepared not so much for what is as for what will be.

FORMATION FOR RELIGIOUS LIFE
TODAY AND TOMORROW

What Is Formation Today?

Formation for religious life is the process by which men and women join a religious congregation; are initiated into its spirituality, life, and mission; and gradually become members of the community. The period before perpetual profession consists of three stages: pre-novitiate, novitiate, and temporary profession. *Directives on Formation in Religious Institutes* states that these three stages together help the new member to grow in spirituality, apostolic life, theology, and the practical living of religious life.

Beginnings

Pre-novitiate may begin with the initial inquiry into the life and works of the community, when a person begins to feel attracted or called to the life, and both the individual and the community begin to explore the possibility. It generally has a more formal stage of living in the community for a period of time, which may be called postulancy or candidacy, or sometimes simply pre-novitiate. Neither of these phases of pre-novitiate is required by canon law, but they may be described in the constitutions of the institute.

The period is a less formal preparation for the novitiate, and a time of deepening discernment and growing relationship between the individual and the community. The individual begins the movement from independence to interdependence with the community. This is a time to determine if the candidate has sufficient human and Christian maturity to enter into the novitiate and also to grow in that maturity. The person may also need this time to adapt to the language and culture of the new community. Those moving more resolutely toward the novitiate generally benefit from the opportunity to experience life in community with members of the congregation and take stock of their affective development and ability to deal with their sexuality in a celibate community lifestyle (no. 43).

Practically speaking, this is a time for individuals to begin living and praying in community with members of the congregation. They will often work, possibly with other members of the congregation. They may take classes in theology or spirituality, if they do not already have this background. There may also be classes or workshops organized by the congregation about its life and spirituality, its history, and its particular way of doing mission, as well as religious life and vows.

Novitiate

The pre-novitiate stage of religious life is focused on discernment and preparing for novitiate, when the formal life of the member in the institute begins. Canon law describes the novitiate as follows:

> The purpose of the novitiate, by which life in an institute begins, is to give the novices a greater understanding of their divine vocation, and of their vocation to that institute. During the novitiate the novices are to experience the manner of life of the institute and form their minds and hearts in its spirit. At the same time their resolution and suitability are to be tested. (canon 646)

The novitiate is a time of integral initiation into the life. The novices receive theoretical and practical instruction in spirituality, theology, and the living of a vowed life in community and ministry. At the same time the novices have sufficient silence and solitude to reflect and pray over all that they are learning, and they have the opportunity to put these values into practice at a time when they are free from other commitments. The novitiate is not a time for academic studies or for full-time professional ministry. Nevertheless, there is room for study and for some experience in ministry. In apostolic communities a second year of novitiate was added to the time of formation to give men and women in their late teens and early twenties a taste of the life of the professed religious on mission. For those entering religious communities after many years of ministry, this may no longer be a necessity.

The novitiate is generally a time of reflection, often gathered with other novices from the same congregation or from the same religious family or with novices from various communities in the local area. Many metro areas organize intercommunity formation programs, particularly for novices. These programs generally cover those subjects that most communities have in common and often invite participants to explore and share the nuances on the subject from their own congregational perspective. Topics covered in these sessions include transitions to novitiate, spirituality of the vows, charisms, commitment, spirituality, and a variety of prayer forms, as well as addictions, sexuality, family systems, tools for self-understanding, and conflict management.

Because men and women often enter their communities in ones and twos these days, the intercommunity experiences afford them the opportunity to share the ups and downs of the formation process with others who are walking the same journey. They can have heart-to-heart talks about their experiences in becoming members of their respective groups.

Novitiate also affords time for one-on-one meetings with the novice director aimed at helping the novices integrate their experiences and ensuring that they get what they need to prepare them for profession and life in the institute. The 1983 document *Essential Elements in the Church's Teaching on Religious Life as Applied to Institutes Dedicated to Works of the Apostolate* describes the role of the novice director as "discernment of God's action; the accompaniment of the religious in the ways of God; the nourishing of life with solid doctrine and the practice of prayer; and, particularly in the first stage, the evaluation of the journey thus far made" (no. 47).

Temporary Profession
Directives on Formation in Religious Institutes says:

> First profession inaugurates a new phase of formation, which benefits from the dynamism and stability derived from profession. For the religious, it is a matter of reaping the fruits of the preceding stages, and of pursuing their own human and spiritual growth. (no. 59)

The newly professed member takes leave of the novitiate and becomes more engaged in the ordinary life of the institute. He or she has the opportunity to put into practice the learning and formational experiences of the novitiate with less direct supervision and support. Vatican II put increased emphasis on the period of temporary profession as a time to enhance the professional and ministerial competence of the new members. However, this is the final period of the initial formation process and both studies and ministry should assist the newly professed in his or her growing integration in the community. It helps the individual move toward total self-donation in response to the call of God, and toward that definitive profession which is an outward witness to this call and response.

Formation into What Is

Historically, the three steps described above have been part of the formation process for at least one hundred years, but they have not been used throughout the Christian centuries. The novitiate is the oldest phase of the process, and evidence of this process dates back to the earliest records of religious life. Temporary profession is a somewhat more recent innovation having been documented for a few hundred years. It is not mentioned in the rules of Saint Benedict, Saint Francis, or Saint Dominic. The phase before novitiate is the most recent addition to the formation process, at least in the extended form that is used now, lasting six months to a year, and sometimes longer.

In the early twentieth century the formation process was highly regimented. Men and women entered with nothing and very soon took on a simplified version of the institute's habit for their postulancy. They learned the schedule, prayers, and customs of the community, and accustomed themselves to the rigors of meticulous conformity. In addition, many recount stories of cleaning, gardening, learning to wear and care for elaborate habits, and caring for elderly religious. Having learned to conform their behavior to the community standards, the novitiate was a time to study religious subjects, practice the vows and learn the history of the religious life. Many religious got their first taste of ministry after their first profession, when they were assigned, generally without their consultation, to a ministry of the community. They were mentored in their ministry by the veteran religious with whom they ministered. After some years they returned to the motherhouse for final vows, often preceded by a preparation that lasted several weeks or months. The entire formation process occurred within one's own institute, with the possible exception that women's communities often invited priests to teach the sisters some of the theology courses.

After Vatican II formation plans were revised in several important ways. First, the council document *Perfectae Caritatis* prohibited novices from being sent out for ministry without first being suitably prepared through courses of study and other professional experience (no. 18). Its implementing document, Pope Paul VI's *Motu Proprio Ecclesiae Sanctae*, further recommended that formation programs of the various religious institutes collaborate in developing courses and programs for their members (no. 37). In addition to these changes, religious institutes were reevaluating many of the details of clothing, schedule, and custom that were out of step with contemporary society. Those in formation had spent a good deal of their time learning and becoming accustomed to all these minutiae, many of which dated back centuries. With these things left aside, formation programs lost part of their content, and both directors and those in formation took some time to adjust to these changes.

Formation in the late twentieth and early twenty-first centuries provides newcomers with a theoretical introduction to the history and practice of religious life as well as with the experience and practice of the life. Current formation programs often seek to find the ideal community to nurture the new member at a time when there are fewer and fewer communities to choose from, and fewer and fewer communities where the life of the member can be sustained after final profession. In addition, they try to fit the current program to an increasingly diverse group of candidates coming to religious life. Those joining religious institutes today come from several age cohorts, with a rich diversity of life experience and professional credentials. They have varied assets, from bank accounts to portfolios to real estate. They have assorted liabilities, from education loans to credit-card debt to pending litigation. They come from across the globe and speak a multitude of languages. They may be young or old, healthy or handicapped; they may be living with health conditions unknown a century ago. These factors highlight both the richness of new members and the challenges of bringing them into membership.

It is difficult to provide an introduction to the spiritual life that is suitable for men and women in their forties and fifties who are entering religious life after having developed their own spirituality for decades. For that matter, it may be a greater challenge to provide an introduction suited to the needs and mentality of men and women in their twenties and thirties, because of the distinctly different cultural background of these candidates.

Most religious recount contact with members of their communities as the most important factor in drawing them into religious life. In a recent discussion about religious life, vocation, and community, many of those participating pointed nostalgically to their best moments in community and the reasons they were drawn to community in the first place. Most of their stories went back fifty years as sisters discussed the care and kindness of members of the community, how they treated one another and those to whom they ministered. This is what drew them to community and kept them. These opportunities to live in active communities and grow into religious life among peers are becoming almost impossible to find. Some religious communities are turning to professional marketing techniques in their vocation programs to get the message out. They are also employing lay vocation directors because no one in the institute is willing or able to take on this role. Would it not be more appropriate to put these energies into facilitating the formation of small vibrant communities that could attract new members by the witness of their lives?

Incorporation into the New

All of this brings us to the discussion of formation for religious life today and formation for what is emerging. Perhaps in every age the best formation for religious life has been the life itself. It calls us into communities to live and grow in our values of gospel living, zeal for mission, deepening spirituality, and mutual support in community. An important part of the new formation will be the ability and willingness of small local communities to invite people into their midst to share life together as they ask themselves and the community they join whether or not God might be calling them to religious life. This will not be the work of specialist vocation directors but of any community willing and able to welcome new members.

As the movement grows, small, local communities can come into networks in which they will coordinate activities when doing so makes sense. One of the areas in which coordination may make sense is in welcoming new members and engaging other local communities in the discernment process. It may help those joining to visit various communities and find the one that best fits their own personal call. The network may also have certain members who are more gifted in welcoming new members and assisting in their discernment. It may also be helpful for inquirers of the same region or age cohort to network, to meet periodically, and to connect online.

Inquirers may be offered a time of living with the community. This should be sufficiently long for them to understand the life of the community and to have enough practical experience to be able to make an initial decision about whether or not to continue in the process. This "long-term visit" or "residency" is analogous to the pre-novitiate stage in religious life, lasting six to twelve months. In addition to those who are clearly choosing the life, it may be that these communities, once they have gained a certain stability and maturity, may be able to welcome long-term sojourners, those who may wish to spend several years in the community as they continue to grow and mature and discern their own call. Some of these may continue with the community; others may find that they benefited from some years in the community but then choose to move away. This flexibility with inquirers will require maturity, discernment, and clarity about boundaries and expectations. These elements have been found to be a benefit to intentional communities and to movements like the Catholic Worker and L'Arche.

The traditional novitiate has been a time when candidates for religious life formally enter into the process of becoming members. It begins with the candidate's request for admission and the affirmation by the receiving community that there seems to be a good fit between the individual and the community with its particular experience of God, community, and mission, and that the individual shows promise of becoming a member of the community. The novitiate provides the candidate with a more formal systematic time of prayer, study, and experience of religious life and mission. Often this is carried out in a particular house of the community, sometimes with other novices, when this is possible. One of the criticisms of the current system is that it sets novices aside in "hot house" communities where life is very different from the life of the community at large. When novices leave the novitiate, there may not be communities where they can integrate themselves in a life-giving way.

The novitiate in emerging smaller and local communities will have a different look and feel. The communities are unlikely to have a separate house to set aside as a novitiate among the houses with which it forms ever broadening networks. Novitiate will have to be lived in the midst of the local community. Candidate and community will engage in mutual discernment, with both having the opportunity for reflection and discernment about the individual's call or vocation and how it can live and flourish in the midst of the local community as members pursue their individual and common vocations. After discernment, the community and the new novice will celebrate a deliberate moment of transition from the informal long-term visit or residency phase into the novitiate.

The community and new novice should also choose a novice director to companion the new novice as he or she moves through the program. In addition, the community, novice, and director will take some time to discuss what will be necessary for this particular novice to enter more deeply into the life of this particular community. How can the community provide a more formal time of prayer, study, and experience of religious life and mission that will enable the novice to grow in his or her vocation and come to a readiness to make a commitment to religious life in this community? Guidelines and frameworks for this discussion will include the areas of prayer and spirituality; the history, theology, and experience of religious life and vows; human maturity and life in community; and celibacy and sexuality. Members of a small, local community will have experience in many of these areas and can plan ways of sharing this with the novice among them. They may take advantage of various networks to enable the novice and the community to have access to a broader range of experts and teachers. Other communities in the network may organize online gatherings of the newer members. They may be able to participate in any intercommunity novitiate programs that are organized in their area. Local colleges, universities, and seminaries may also have programs that can help to broaden the formational experiences of the novice. In short, the novice and the community will have the responsibility of drawing together a coherent program from the resources available to them. In addition to classes, programs, and workshops, the life itself is an invitation. The novice will engage the community as it lives, prays, and works together. The community will grow as the novice comes to discover and engage in the life. As a community of praxis, the community has committed itself to a radical living of the gospel, which attracted the novice in the first place. Sharing in the practical living of the life should continue to nurture the vocation of each member of the community, and all should grow and deepen in personal and community life in Christ.

Through a combination of formal study, prayer, reflection, discernment, and life in community, the novice will grow in his or her personal vocation. Over the period of a year or two, the novice and the community should grow in clarity about the ability of the novice to enter fully into the life of the community and to make a vowed commitment in the community. Like every relationship, it will have its challenges. However, every member should be a blessing to the community, as the community is a blessing to the member as together they live out their vowed commitment.

Once a person has spent sufficient time as a novice, the community again enters into a mutual discernment. If the community members determine that the person is ready, he or she may profess vows for a year or for a period of years. During the period of temporary profession the prayer and study of the novitiate give way to the prayer and study of a professed member. It continues as the new member engages in ministry and in the life of the community, up to the day when he or she is ready to make a permanent commitment to vowed life in the community.

If the life continues to develop as a network of communities, it may be helpful for the new member to spend some time in another community of the network. This experience could be mutually enriching as the new member gains a broader experience of religious life, and the new member broadens the experience of the second community. New members in the second community will also have the opportunity to share their experience of formation, and the new members can support one another as they grow into the life of their communities.

As with other postmodern groupings, everyone will have to take care to clarify expectations and ensure that each member is free to come into community and to settle into the community he or she finds life giving. At the same time, everyone should be cognizant of certain mutual obligations within the network so that there is a sense that all the communities are strengthened as each is strengthened. As the movement grows, it will be necessary to clarify how one makes a permanent commitment in the local community and becomes part of the larger movement. Historically, communities have been able to afford sufficient autonomy to local regions, provinces, or monasteries to accept, form, and incorporate new members who became members of the larger congregation or order. The present model envisions a world in which the local communities would be smaller and the network looser. As a new member comes, the community can discern with him or her when and how these experiences in other communities would be most helpful. In addition, the possibilities of other communities in the network hosting a new member will have to be taken into account. It may also be helpful for religious of the same chronological age, or of the same time in community, to gather periodically on a regional level for retreat and renewal.

This chapter has attempted to peer into the future and imagine how emerging religious life will look. It has explored how religious life will organize itself, and how it will go about the task of welcoming and incorporating new members. As with any emergence, it will take energy, imagination, and patience to develop new ways of being together in a new life form that is smaller, more local, and more autonomous than religious life of the twentieth century. It is another task to begin to create these structures and to move from where we are today in religious life into the structures that will nurture and sustain its future. The task is just beginning, and there is a growing awareness that it is time to begin with those who are currently coming to religious communities to join in the tremendous adventure that is religious life.

MYSTICS AND PROPHETS

Religious life is as diverse as the human story. It has built empires and challenged corrupt systems of power. It has educated,
healed, comforted. In its best moments religious men and
women have fed the hungry, healed the sick, educated children,
comforted the sorrowing, and accompanied the dying. They
have lived and taught the gospel and contended with every manner of anti-gospel force. In its worst moments religious men and
women have probably committed every sin in the books and
colluded with systems of power and oppression. They have lied,
stolen, raped, pillaged, plundered, and betrayed the trust placed
in them by church and society, and by the weak and powerless
they aspired to serve. At its core, religious life is a life form that
aspires to the best in the human spirit; it gathers and nurtures
mystics and prophets.

MYSTICS

When I speak of mysticism, I am not speaking of esoteric spirituality or visions of angels, nor am I speaking of some psychic
state induced by a combination of drugs, alcohol and mental
illness. I am speaking of a profound spirituality that is the call of
every Christian, indeed, of every human person. To be human
is to be open to the Divine, sensitive to the sacred all around
us, within us, and between us. God who is Love creates out of
Love and makes us in the image of Love. Our deepest truth is
an openness to this God of love. Some of us are sensitive to

religious images and symbols and find the Divine in scripture, prayer, and liturgy. But those who are not sensitive to religious images are created in the image of God and share this fundamental openness to the transcendent and ultimately to God. Everyone can nourish the God image within; all can nurture their contemplative side. The human spirit is open to beauty, to art, to nature, to service, to goodness, to truth, to love. When we are overwhelmed by goodness, truth or beauty, when words fail, when our spirit breathes forth a Wow!, we are on holy ground; we are touching the face of God.

By *mysticism* I mean a spirituality that surrenders completely and explicitly to the Divine and to the work of a God who is Love. God loves by creating and creates by loving. Mystics surrender to this *opus dei*, this work of God, the divine project. They surrender in their own lives to the work of God's creative Love.

> Yea, thy gazes, blissful lover,
> Make the beauties they discover.[1]

Religious life is deliberately and explicitly oriented to nurturing and fostering this life of the spirit through prayer, spirituality, vows, community, and mission. Each of these elements contributes to making the life what it is, a life that always points beyond itself, just as the human spirit always points beyond itself.

Religious life has a fundamental orientation to prayer and attention to the sacred. Spirituality is attending to the sacred and understanding its dynamics; it is articulating and sharing the experience of the sacred. Vows open a place in our hearts, in our lives, and in our communities. They open a space for the sacred. They are deliberately directed to the sacred and to fostering our spirituality and to nurturing the community within which that spirituality grows and matures.

Communities support, sustain, and nurture sacred space and create a place to welcome and initiate newcomers into the

---

[1] Francis Thompson, "Mistress of Vision," in *The Works of Francis Thompson*, 3 vols. (London: Burns and Oates, 1913), 2:22.

life of the spirit. As our spirits rest in this sacred space, they are recreated in the image of God, this God who is Love. As John of Ruysbroeck wrote in the fourteenth century:

> And therefrom follows the last point that can be put into words, that is, when the spirit beholds a Darkness into which it cannot enter with the reason. And there it feels itself dead and lost to itself, and one with God without difference and without distinction. And when it feels itself one with God, then God Himself is its peace and its enjoyment and its rest. And this is an unfathomable abyss wherein man must die to himself in blessedness, and must live again in virtues, whenever love and its stirring demand it.[2]

I am not unaware of the challenge of speaking about mysticism and avoiding the reduction of the deepest spirituality to some form of pantheism. This is a risk of every mystic in the history of the church. But we can't for this reason speak only of a God that is limited to temples made by human hands or to theologies that fit neatly into human minds. "Even Satan disguises himself as an angel of light" (2 Cor 11:14), but there are still angels of light out there. And we would not do well to avoid angels of light, for fear some might be malicious spirits. Careful discernment, spiritual direction, and wise spiritual guides are of immense help in this realm. Personal honesty and humility coupled with a selfless reliance on the God Who Is, the God who is Love, will allow us to seek and follow the counsel that will lead us through these "mine fields." Paul urges the Corinthians to "pursue love and strive for the spiritual gifts, and especially that you may prophesy . . . [for] those who prophesy speak to other people for their upbuilding and encouragement and consolation" (1 Cor 14:1, 3). The author of the *Cloud of*

---

[2] John of Ruysbroeck, "Sparkling Stone," in *The Adornment of the Spiritual Marriage*, ed. Evelyn Underhill, trans. C. A. Wynschenk (London: J. M. Dent and Sons, 1916), Chap. XIII.

Unknowing reiterates this: "And so I urge you, go after experience rather than knowledge. On account of pride, knowledge may often deceive you, but this gentle, loving affection will not deceive you. Knowledge tends to breed conceit, but love builds. Knowledge is full of labor, but love, full of rest."[3]

PROPHETS

The life of prophecy is also fundamental to religious life. From deep immersion in the Divine that we call mysticism, we surrender to the project of God within our own lives and in the world around us. God's plan in our own life is not a separate project from the plan God has for the world—there is only one plan. God is Love, God creates by loving, God loves by creating. God is always bringing forth life, love, and goodness.

Captured by the heart of the Divine, we are captured by a God who goes out in love and gentleness, healing and tenderness for all that is. Surrendering to the divine project also means that the gospel is my story—I tell it not as the words of an ancient itinerant prophet, but as a story about Divine Love that resonates in my own heart. "Woe betide me if I do not proclaim the gospel" (1 Cor 9:16). It is my own deepest truth.

> The man who is sent down by God from these heights into the world is full of truth and rich in all virtues. And he seeks not his own but the glory of Him Who has sent him. And hence he is just and truthful in all things, and he possesses a rich and a generous ground, which is set in the richness of God: and therefore he must always spend himself on those who have need of him; for the living fount of the Holy Ghost, which is his wealth, can never be spent.[4]

---

[3] William Johnston, ed., *The Cloud of Unknowing and The Book of Privy Counseling* (Garden City, NY: Image Books, 1973), 188.

[4] Ruysbroeck, "Sparkling Stone," Chap. XIV.

The mystics must prophesy because they have been filled to overflowing by the God of Love. Their words, their works, and their lives flow through their hearts from their source in the heart of God. They still trod the ways of earth, they still get entangled in the daily affairs of the task, they weaken and fall, and they always fall short of their desires. But there is a fire in their hearts that cannot be quenched or overcome (Jer 20:9). Yet that deepest core of their existence pulsates with the fire of divine love: "My grace is sufficient for you, for power is made perfect in weakness" (2 Cor 12:9).

COMMUNITIES OF MYSTICS AND PROPHETS

All of Christian life aspires to mysticism and prophecy, all of human life is open to it. But it is religious life that is deliberately and purposefully oriented to mysticism and prophecy. In each age when the life reinvented itself, this happened not in board rooms or in the halls of power, but in hearts immersed in the Divine. Religious life with its consecration, community, and mission has been honed over the centuries to balance those elements that have proven helpful in building up communities of mystics and prophets. It is these men and women who have accomplished the great works of religious communities, the missionary expansion, networks of schools and universities, and systems of hospitals and clinics. They are like a great old tree whose roots sink deep into the soil to nourish its sprawling branches. Its strength is possible only because of its deep rootedness in the Divine.

Religious life is a primary life commitment, to the exclusion of any other primary life commitment. For this reason members focus their life's energy on spiritual depth and evangelical fruitfulness, on mysticism and prophecy. They occupy a particular place in the community of faith and "from everyone to whom much has been given, much will be required" (Lk 12:48). Their lives, more than their works, are the gift they share with the community of faith as they seek to incarnate the God of love in the community of faith and in the world at large.

EMERGING RELIGIOUS LIFE

The current situation of religious life, the church from which it springs, and contemporary society all point to the emergence of a new form of religious life. Those in and around religious life have known for decades that something new was coming, and we have strained the "eyes of our hearts" to catch a glimpse of what it might look like. We knew that this new development was beyond our imagination but that when it finally appeared, it would do honor to the heritage of religious life. The day is finally dawning, and the new form is beginning to emerge in our spirits, imaginations, and conversations. The reinvention of religious life for today is a renewed commitment to the choice of radical Christian community that inspired, attracted, and sustained the religious of every age. We will discover anew how to live the beatitudes in a deliberate way. We may take inspiration from the New Monasticism movement, which has sought to commit to these same values in the evangelical context. Its twelve marks are a good point of departure in imagining the life we hope to live. In this way we can be a blessing to those who have come before us in the life, as well as a blessing for the wider Christian community and the world at large.

In community, we all face our personal darkness, which can come out in community. The weakest has strengths, the strongest has weakness. Together we set out to make a path by our collective footsteps; it is a road that never ends but winds through history, sometimes on broad open roads, sometimes by narrow footpaths. Many will come to see if this is their path, if they can live with the ambiguity, if they can risk their lives on the path. Some will know this is their heart's journey and in freedom can give a wholehearted response.

Jesus' story can never be captured by reading it alone. Others come to know it in the breaking of the bread and in the sharing of our lives together when we gather in Jesus' name. Jesus is the foundation, the gospel is the task, and community is the process. In small, local communities we can share life that is undifferentiated, immediate, and egalitarian. These communities can network to share services while affording each community the freedom and versatility to adapt to its local reality. Resisting the drive toward centralization, they can become circles of gospel living, peace, and justice. They can be mystics and prophets in a world desperately in need of them.

INDEX